Center Stage

By Dannye Williamsen

Published by:
Williamsen Publications
Memphis, TN

http://www.WilliamsenPublications.com
http://www.DannyeWilliamsen.com

ISBN: 978-0-9726058-3-0

Dedication

This story is dedicated to the people in my life
who have always allowed for the possibility
of my personal growth before jumping to conclusions
based on the person I might have been at one time.

Chapter 1

The shades rested cockeyed at the top of the window frames, the cords curled up on the sills with the curtains hanging indifferently along the edges of the window. The morning sun lit up the room, exposing at least a month's layer of dust on the dresser and the bedside table. Cobwebs hung in all the corners. At first glance one would think no one had been here in quite a while, but you'd be wrong. Somewhere under the comforter and the huge pile of blankets was the owner of this seemingly forsaken refuge.

As the warm rays of the sun seeped through her coverings, April attempted to rise to meet the day, expecting her life to have changed while she was in that ephemeral sleep. Looking out through the windows, she saw the fields where the corn stalks were knee-high now. Of course! It was nearly the fourth of July. She'd been hearing that since she was a child. *The corn should be knee-high by the fourth of July or the crop's in trouble!* She had no idea if it was true or not, but she always expected to see the fields green with corn when the fireworks met the sky in July.

The air was humid. April knew she needed to raise the windows and turn on the attic fan unless she planned to fry by midday, but she couldn't seem to move. Her body felt heavy, though she probably only weighed one hundred and ten pounds. She'd been much heavier in the past, but in the last few years she'd lost a lot of weight, among other things. This morning it seemed all the things she had lost, including her weight, had returned and were crushing the very life out of her. Her efforts to rise, to sling her feet off the bed and onto the floor, went unnoticed. There was no connection between her body and her mind. After a few minutes April gave in, rolling her head sideways to look out the window again.

She recognized the symptoms. She had experienced them many times over her lifetime. She didn't need a doctor to tell her depression was setting in for the long haul. What she needed was a doctor to do something about it! April's respect for doctors lay somewhere between her disdain for slugs and her hatred of rats. In the last few years, the bouts of depression had hit hard and often. The doctors had done nothing. April guessed it was God's way of balancing the scales. Diagnosed as a "manic-depressive" years back, April had seemed more manic than depressed most of the time.

Just didn't have time for depression back then, she thought. *Now, what else is there to do?*

April's thoughts wandered to her childhood. Her family were all gone now: her mother and father, her sister Dawn, her brother Robert. Robert died first. He had a heart attack at thirty-four. It seemed like it was a century ago. April could barely remember him. As she strained to mentally reconstruct his features, her mind began replaying the time he had tried to teach her to ride a bicycle without training wheels.

"Go slow," he'd hollered as she pedaled faster and faster down the gravel driveway. April had heard him, but it seemed like such silly advice as the air blew through her hair. She just knew she would lift off the ground at any second. Just before reaching the roadway, she braked hard. The bicycle slid, and gravel flew into the air. Half an hour later, her cuts and bruises had been tended, and she was in the backyard showing Robert her wounds.

"I told you to go slow," he said.

With her eyes wide, April asked, "Why? Going fast was fun!" Robert just shrugged, not bothering to answer her question. Thinking back, she realized it was the only time she could remember his showing any concern whatsoever for her.

Not heeding Robert's advice was a decision that appeared to define the rest of her life. She'd always ignored the advice of those who really cared about her until they finally left, exhausted by the effort. Now she was alone. The funny thing, she repeatedly told herself, was that being alone was always the thing she secretly feared the most. Now she was nearing the downhill side of her life, and there was no one. No one to call. No one at all, not even an acquaintance she could pretend was a friend. Even her ex-husband and her daughter were no longer around.

"Where did everyone go?" April asked aloud as the first bead of sweat trickled across her forehead, following the path nature had provided until it dropped unceremoniously onto the pillow.

Chapter 2

At The Crossroads Restaurant

"What!?" April grumbled. Who could possibly be banging on her door at this time of the morning, she thought as she slowly rolled onto her side. "Go away!" she complained. "Just leave me alone." The banging did not stop. It continued with only short intervals between. Lying there, April was appalled to realize that the knocking was now a tune. Next she'd be hearing the raspy sounds of a washboard accompanied by a jug band if she didn't put an end to this.

With renewed purpose, she sat up on the side of the bed and slipped her feet into her house shoes. Grabbing a robe on her way out of the bedroom, she moved with more determination than she had exhibited in a long while to confront this person who was disturbing her misery. Prepared to hit her intruder with a barrage of words to scald his ears, April jerked the door open. "Wha—" she began but was struck dumb by the sight standing in front of her. It was a woman. At least she thought it was a woman. The way she was dressed, she could be an hallucination, a remnant left over from a fairy tale about gingerbread houses and kindly old grandmothers. She actually had on a pinafore!

"Good morning, sweetie! I brought you these muffins for breakfast. I thought we'd sit down with a cup of coffee and get to know each other." With a look of concern, the woman added, "My! You look like you need more than a muffin and coffee, but it's a start, dearie." She shrugged and moved past April into the house. "Which way to the kitchen?"

Before April could respond, the woman headed off to the right with muffin basket in hand. Speechless, April pushed the door closed and followed her. Coming into the kitchen, she watched as the woman cleared off the kitchen table and began setting out plates and fixing coffee as if she had lived here all her life. Her brief spurt of energy exhausted, April plopped down on a chair, waiting to see what fate had in store for her now.

April looked at the muffin the woman placed in front of her. She tentatively reached out to touch it with her finger. She wanted to make sure it was real because otherwise, this was one hell of a bad trip. She hadn't thought her meds were capable of creating hallucinations, but maybe she'd gotten hold of some of those black market prescription drugs they'd been warning about on TV. Her finger touched the muffin. It was still warm. Her stomach growled in response.

"Go ahead, eat it. Lord knows you need it," the woman declared.

Taking a bite, April could barely keep herself from moaning with pleasure. After a few more bites, she looked directly at this strange woman and inquired, "Should I know you?"

"Of course not!" she replied with a chuckle. "I just arrived this week. Want another muffin?" she asked, placing another on April's plate without waiting for an answer.

"Do you always bake muffins for your neighbors?" April asked. She knew it was a stupid question, but she was having a bit of trouble gathering her thoughts into a coherent stream.

"Only for very special ones."

Taken aback by her odd response, April asked, "Do you have a name?"

"Don't you?" the woman asked, the corner of her mouth tilting upward.

Flustered, April replied, "I meant what is your name?"

"Well, why didn't you say so? My name is Grace. It's what is known as a virtue name."

"A virtue name?"

"Yes. People have been giving their children virtue names for centuries. They believe they can protect their children from negative influences by bestowing a name which might imbue them with that virtue. Grace means *the state of being in God's favor.* Do you know what April means?"

"The month?" replied April, suddenly feeling very stupid.

Chuckling, Grace answered, "Well, of course, that's what most people think of, but it comes from the Latin *aperire* which means *to open,* like the opening of flowers."

"Oh" was the only response April could muster because she had no idea where this conversation was going.

"What do you think the opening of flowers has to do with you?" Grace poured more coffee into April's cup as she waited for an answer. Since April had no idea, she chose to say nothing. Smiling, Grace continued, "Flowers, my dear, open themselves up, giving of themselves to the world and taking from it only what they need to allow their beauty to shine forth. Where else can you find such a perfect give and take? Where else can you find such perfect beauty than among the flowers? It starts you to thinking, doesn't it?"

It starts me to thinking you're a nutcase, thought April. She decided that if she could just finish her coffee, she would let this woman, Grace, know politely that she needed to get dressed, and perhaps then she would leave.

"Of course, you should get dressed, dear. It would be a wonderful change of pace for you!" Grace said, a broad smile on her face.

April was sure she had not spoken a word aloud. Or had she? Seizing the opportunity, however, she replied, "Yes, I do. If you would excuse me then" as she rose from the chair.

"Certainly. I'll just clean up in here, and when you're ready, we'll head out."

"Head out?" April was no longer sure she wasn't in the middle of some kind of depressive hysteria. Maybe not emotionally, but circumstances definitely seemed to be out of her control. For the first time, she wondered if it was time to do something about the depression she'd allowed herself to wallow in for the last few months. Maybe she should visit her doctor, get a new prescription, and actually *take* the prescription regularly.

"Yes, it's time you got out of the house and reconnected with the world out there—"

"But, how do you…" April paused, desperately trying to figure out who this woman really was.

"Sweetie, it's not difficult to see that you've been hiding out here for a while. You need to get out," nodding toward the hair sticking out in all directions on April's head.

Incensed, April replied, "I have not been hiding out!"

"Well, whatever you call it, dear, it hasn't been good for your complexion. Now, get along and get cleaned up."

Totally nonplussed, April minded Grace as a child would a parent.

April rummaged in her purse for her sunglasses as she walked down the steps toward the driveway. "Where the hell are they?" she muttered.

"Try the back pocket, dear," replied Grace.

Looking askance at her, April flipped the flap over the main pockets of her purse and unzipped the back pocket. To her consternation, there they were. "How did you—"

Grace tossed her hand dismissively in the air. "Well, it just stood to reason. You'd looked everywhere else."

Not convinced that was how she knew, April nevertheless shrugged it off. "I take it we're going in my car," she remarked.

"Of course, dear. I don't drive anymore unless it's absolutely necessary."

Sighing, April unlocked the car doors and plopped down in the driver's seat. "Where to?" she asked as she pulled out of the driveway and headed toward town. How did she get herself in this situation, she wondered. She felt like Dorothy in *The Wizard of Oz*. Perhaps she'd fallen asleep and woken up in an alternate universe — one where the 1950s were still going on. Glancing toward Grace, it was impossible to imagine anyone in the 21st century dressing like that. Who wore frilly dresses and pinafores these days? As a matter of fact, the last time she'd seen anyone wearing anything close to Grace's getup *was* Dorothy in *The Wizard of Oz*!

"Turn here, dear," Grace said, pointing to the left. April obeyed. "There! There's a perfect parking place just over there." Pulling in along the curb, April had given up asking where they were going. Obviously the fates had something in mind for her so it was out of her hands.

Unbuckling her seat belt, Grace remarked, "You know, April, I've always thought it was wonderful the way we always have choices.

Don't you think that's wonderful?" April just stared at her. Was it possible this woman was psychic? Before she could come to a conclusion though, Grace was tapping on the top of the car for her to get out. *Who the hell is this woman, and what the hell am I doing following her around?* April asked herself, but she'd been depressed for so long, she wasn't sure she was strong enough to stand up to her. With a sigh, she stepped out of the car and locked it.

Looking around at this unfamiliar part of town, April felt uncomfortable. It wasn't that drug dealers were lurking on the corners or anything like that; it was just so different. The buildings were pre-1900, but they had been updated in the last century—just not in this century. She spotted a couple of quaint restaurants and assumed that's where Grace was headed. One was called The Feeding Trough and the other Alice's Tea Room. *Please let it be Alice's*, she thought. When they passed The Feeding Trough, she sighed in relief, but her relief was short-lived when Grace suddenly made a sharp right turn down the alley between the two buildings.

"Where are we going?" April demanded. She was starting to wonder if the frilly dress and pinafore were a clever disguise for a ruthless criminal of some kind. After all, she didn't even know the woman's last name for cripes' sake and here she was, following her around like a puppy dog.

"It's all right, dear. We're almost there."

"Almost where?"

"You'll see soon enough," Grace answered when she reached the end of the alley. April could see nothing but a small, barren clearing and a stand of trees. She could just barely see the river through the trees on her left. Without hesitation, Grace began walking rather oddly across the dusty clearing. Looking closely, April realized she was walking on stepping stones carefully placed in the ground and almost invisible. Glancing behind her into the alley, April quickly followed Grace across the clearing.

"Damn! I wish I had remembered to bring my gun," April said to Grace's back.

"What?!" Grace stopped and turned to face April.

Pointing toward the woods, April replied, "I mean, if we're going to have to hunt for our lunch, it would be easier if I had a gun."

Shaking her head, Grace laughed. "At least you still have a sense of humor."

"What does that mean?"

Turning, Grace started walking down the stone-marked path again. "Well, you have to admit you haven't been a bundle of laughs so far." Pointing, she added, "It's not much farther, just around these trees."

April didn't reply. She was still stinging from her earlier remark. She did so have a sense of humor. Okay, so she hadn't utilized it much lately, but it didn't mean she didn't have one.

Just as Grace cleared the trees, she remarked, "Everyone has a sense of humor, my dear. It's just that some seem to be saving it for a rainy day. The one trait which comes to us unchanged from God is a sense of humor, the ability to laugh. Ah, here we are."

April looked up to see an old house perched next to the river. It was dark brown, but she couldn't tell from here if it was painted or just weathered. There were few windows on this side of the house, but there was a door. It had an awning over the stoop the way many old-style restaurants did with The Crossroads imprinted on it.

"Is this a restaurant?" she asked.

"Of course, dear. Where did you think we were going?" Grace replied.

To be honest, April thought, she'd had no idea where they were going, and now that they were here, she still wasn't sure. "I've never heard of this place, and it's not exactly on the beaten path." At that moment she saw the sign on the front door: Invitation Only. "Are they expecting us?" she asked, nodding at the sign.

"Oh, yes. Definitely." Grace opened the door and walked in. There was no one in the foyer. Grace did not wait. She strolled through the foyer into the adjoining room as if it were hers. April looked around at the walls covered in books. Couches sat at angles all around the room in an attempt, it seemed, to provide privacy to each. What the heck was this place?

"Come on, dear," Grace said, motioning for April to follow her down a hallway. They stepped out onto a large enclosed deck overlooking the river. Only five tables were set up on the deck. Two huge ceiling fans, one at each end of the deck, were turning rapidly, creating a comfortable environment despite the summer heat. Grace headed for the table closest to the river.

Once they were seated, a waiter materialized — at least that was what it seemed like to April. "Would you ladies like something cool to drink on this warm day?"

"Without a doubt, Henry!" replied Grace. "I'll have your wonderfully sweet tea with no lemon, please. How about you, dear?"

April didn't reply. She was still fighting with herself over whether this was all an hallucination or a dream. Was she still in her bed? Had she been mesmerized by the stalks of corn in the field and the heat and slipped back into a dream state?

"Just bring her a sweet tea, also, Henry. She's been a bit under the weather lately. A little sweetness will do her good." Henry nodded knowingly and walked away.

"Am I asleep?" April asked as she surreptitiously pinched herself under the table. "Ouch!" she remarked before she could stop herself.

"You really shouldn't go around pinching yourself, dear. It causes bruises," Grace replied, reaching across the table to pat April's hand. "Are you asleep? Of course not! I'm not asleep so how on earth could I have gotten you here if you were asleep?" Chuckling, she added, "However, in a lot of ways, you have been asleep for a long time, and maybe it's time you woke up."

Confused for sure now, April gazed at this ridiculously clad woman and wondered if she had truly lost her mind. This was just too weird to be true. If she wasn't asleep, then she must be on some kind of bad trip. Who dreams up an old woman wearing a pinafore and a restaurant that's "invitation only?" No one would unless they were flying high.

"Oh my! If I had known my outfit would upset you so much, I would have chosen something more suitable. It's my fault. I just love wearing dresses, and pinafores are just so handy. Oh, I know it's out of style, but I was never one to be influenced by the trend of the day."

Of course not, thought April. "Just exactly who—"

"But rest assured I am just as real as you are," Grace interrupted. "We've been looking at your life, April, and it's so sad to see someone who has taken such promise and twisted it and distorted it until in the end, she is even more damaged than those she has betrayed."

Stunned into silence, April simply stared. Totally against her will, visions of her life were flowing rapidly through her mind. She was shocked to realize that instead of seeing her past glories, she was seeing a series of events where she was the villain. As her mind travelled down this road, she saw bodies lying to the side, either maimed or dying. "Who are you?" she screamed at Grace, disrupting the visions. "None of that was true! I've done great things in my life. A lot of people have become rich and famous because of me. Sure, things are a little tough right now, but I'll come back. I always do."

Grace shook her head. "With perhaps one exception, the bodies were simply metaphorical in order to get your attention, April dear. However, would you really like to know what has happened to the people in your life? You've never looked back. As soon as you got what you wanted, you left them behind without regard for the consequences of your actions."

"That's not true!" she shouted so loudly that the waiter, who had arrived with their tea, nearly dropped the glasses. "Sorry," she mumbled. Nodding, he set the glasses down and retreated.

Before she could speak, the visions began again, only this time they reached back into her childhood with quick glimpses of broken people whom she had betrayed or discounted on her way to whatever she wanted. She involuntarily shuddered.

"Is this the legacy you want to leave behind?" Grace intruded on her vision.

"Uh, I don't think ... are you sure ... that can't be true!" Feelings which had never entered her emotional experience before — regret, compassion, shame — were flooding through April. She didn't know how to cope with these strange sentiments. Her world had never allowed for concern about the consequences for other people. The aftereffects were their problem. If they weren't savvy enough to take care of themselves, it wasn't her fault. Suddenly she was finding it difficult to breathe. What the hell?

"Oh, but, dear, it is your responsibility," Grace interrupted her thoughts.

"No, it isn't!" she insisted. "Was it wrong for me to try and better myself?" A strange sensation was causing her arms and fingers to tingle. Was she having a stroke? *Great!* she thought. *What a way to go!*

"No, but it wasn't the best choice to try to do it at the expense of others — and you're not having a stroke so don't worry."

April, who had been staring at her hands like they belonged to someone else, jerked her head up to stare instead at Grace. "Who the hell are you? Don't tell me you're just some sweet little lady who's trying to be nice to me because I don't buy it! You've been reading my mind — no! Don't argue with me. I know I didn't say that about a stroke out loud. So who are you, lady?" April shouted, pushing her chair back to tower over Grace.

Undisturbed by April's aggressive act, Grace said, "Sit down, dear. We have things to discuss." Deflating like a balloon, April plopped back onto the chair, propped her elbows on the table, and hid her face behind her hands. "Now, now. Pull yourself together. I have a job for you." April raised her head. "I want you to take your time and think back over the things you've done in your life. I don't want you to fight these new feelings you're having because they are the key to changing everything for you. Do you think you can do this?"

April shrugged. "Why?" she asked. "There's nothing I can do to change it, and until a few minutes ago wouldn't have even wanted to." She could hear her words and feel the regret attached to them. There was still a foreign quality to this feeling of regret, like it belonged to someone else. Perhaps it wasn't permanent, only a passing fancy.

"Oh, it's not so new," remarked Grace, once again startling April by reading her mind. "You've felt regret in the past but only when it related to something *you* lost. Feels different when you step outside your own narcissistic realm, doesn't it, even if only for a few moments?"

April started to object to such slander but quickly sensed it was true. "Again, what difference can rehashing it make?" She needed to sleep. This was all making her very tired. Her eyes drooped, and she felt them cross in an effort to regain control.

"Close your eyes and sit quietly. Allow yourself to just observe, dear." Grace watched as April's eyes closed and her shoulders relaxed. "Now examine your life with new eyes. You will be able to see the lives of others as they related to your path. Find that one place in time where you could have made a different choice and your life would have gone down a better path. It won't necessarily be at the beginning. No one lives a life without regrets, but there is always a point where we get so far away from our heartsong we can no longer even hear the notes."

"Ummm," muttered April. She couldn't remember ever being this relaxed. It was better than any meds she'd ever taken. *Need to find out what they put in that tea,* she thought just before her mind released the present and slipped without fanfare into the past.

Chapter 3

Brandon Foster

Location. Location. Location. She never thought she would say that about a desk, but in this case, it was true. No one could see her from their offices, but she could hear them coming down the hall. Consequently, she could fool around as much as she wanted as long as she looked busy when they rounded the corner. She looked out onto the green area, or the mall as the building owners liked to call it. From her vantage point she could see everything that went on in the building. Well, almost everything, and she would certainly see everyone at some point because the restrooms were just past her office.

"April, I want you to work with Rhonda this afternoon. She'll show you how to fill out the reports for the district office. It's pretty straight forward, but it does have to be accurate."

She jerked so hard at the sound of his voice her pen flew out of her hand and rolled across the desk. Norman Croswell had appeared out of nowhere. She didn't understand why she hadn't heard him coming. Looking down, she understood why. He was wearing tennis shoes. Who would have expected that of Norman? *Guess it's casual Tuesday*, she thought.

"Sorry, I didn't hear you come up," she remarked, reaching for her pen.

Not bothering to acknowledge her remark, Norman continued on. "Rhonda should be back from lunch about one o'clock. She's in the first office on the left. Make sure you transfer the incoming calls to her phone so you can answer them while you're there." He then disappeared as abruptly as he'd arrived.

What a jerk! I bet he wouldn't get excited if I walked into his office, shut the door, and dropped my dress to the floor. Norman might not get excited, but April's pulse was racing just contemplating the possibility. *What a kick*, she thought. The phone rang, and April's thoughts leaped onto a new track with ease and agility. She was nothing if not flexible.

The weeks passed. April quickly became the information banker in the building. If you needed the "goods" on someone, you went to April Saunders to make a withdrawal. Unfortunately, the interest rate for your withdrawal was exorbitant because there was no way to ever finish your business with April. Your need for the information became one of her assets and could just as easily be loaned out to another desperate soul.

April had never anticipated that her receptionist job would turn into such a gold mine. It was perfect! She had few responsibilities except answering the phone and typing a few letters. The rest of the time she dreamed. She dreamed about being a powerful woman with lots of money. She knew she had the talent for being powerful. She was already proving that right here. Nothing happened she didn't know about and didn't use to her advantage. Still, she wanted to be on the top manipulating those beneath her — not on the bottom manipulating those around her and above her. What good was power if you didn't have the goods to show for it?

It was Saturday, and no one was working except April and Brandon Foster, the president of Brandon Foster Investments. It wasn't a financial investment company like April had thought when she applied for the job. It was a land investment and construction company. Brandon had moved into the city from his parents' farm three years earlier. He had been around equipment and dealt with land all his life. He was tired of farming the land; he wanted to build on it.

His dreams took off like a rocket bound for another galaxy. Everyone declared he had the magic touch. In those three years, he had built a company now being sought after by some of the bigger fish in the sea. He had already received eight-figure offers from several investors. Luckily, he was still a privately-owned company. Otherwise, there would have been a flurry of buyers after the stock and a school of sharks after him.

Brandon still had dreams, and they weren't all about the money. It was his responsibility to give his wife and three-year-old daughter the "good life" they deserved. He had known Claire since he was nine years old. He had never dated anyone else. He didn't know if he never wanted to or simply never had. He and Claire had just always been together. His grandmother used to say he and Claire had made a contract to be together before they were born. Up until he was twenty-three, he believed her without even giving it a second thought.

One day he looked in the crib at Amanda. Little brown curls folded around her face, just like Claire's. Struck by the resemblance, he wondered if Claire had looked like Amanda when she was six months old. If he and Claire had been in the same room at that same age, would they have known they had made a contract to be together? Suddenly, it all seemed so silly to him. How could they possibly have made a contract with each other? At that moment, he felt betrayed by his grandmother, by Claire, and by life — as if they had sheltered him from all life had to offer.

For some reason he could not explain, his feelings toward Claire changed that day. He felt guilty about it, and he'd worked even harder to make sure she had everything she could ever want — at least materially. He still loved her. She had been his friend for so long he couldn't imagine being without her, but the flame that had been there, perhaps kindled by his grandmother's words, had subsided into quiet embers.

Confused, Brandon had diverted all the fire of his youth into his dreams, and it had paid off. He would certainly never have to worry about money again, but it didn't keep him from working every opportunity he got. He knew Claire had given up expecting him home for supper or planning family week-ends. If she needed him, she knew he would be at the office. Claire had never hinted at there being another woman, and he had never cheated on her. He was glad she seemed content to continue being his best friend since she had never questioned why they rarely made love anymore. He wouldn't have known what to say if she had.

When Brandon unlocked the back door of the office that Saturday morning, he walked into his office and sat down behind his desk. He tore the top sheet off the desk pad. Monday was a new month. After lining up his stapler and his tape dispenser, he shifted the picture of Claire and Amanda so they weren't looking directly at him.

After a few minutes of shuffling, he again sat quietly behind his desk. He didn't really have anything to do. He just didn't have any place else to go. He picked up the neatly stacked phone messages and thumbed through them. There was only one he really needed to handle. The rest were just people trying to sell him something — equipment, land, a sure-fire deal. He wadded them all into a ball and tossed it at the trash can by the door. The pink ball of paper clipped the rim of the waste basket, propelling it into the hall.

Brandon looked at it a minute. Then he got up slowly and walked toward the door. He bent down to pick up the errant paper ball to throw it into the basket. He couldn't possibly miss this close, but before he could raise himself up and recover his dignity by slam dunking the pink ball, he was startled to find himself staring at a woman's legs. *Nice legs*, he thought. Rising slowly, trying to keep the home court advantage, Brandon realized it was the receptionist, April.

"Hello, uh, April. What are you doing here?"

"Hello, Mr. Foster. Did I startle you?" April had intended to take him by surprise. Her motto was: *Never give anyone warning*. It was best to strike first and strike fast. She was finding this worked in almost any situation. It didn't matter if it was physical or mental. If your prey didn't have time to plan, the odds were stacked in your favor every time.

"Uh…no. I was just...uh...I just missed the waste basket and was picking up the paper." Brandon didn't know why he was explaining himself to her. "What are you doing here, April?" he asked, trying to regain his authority.

"Oh, I had some filing to catch up on. I was so busy Friday getting all those letters typed up for you — you know, the ones to the mortgage company? Anyway, I got behind, and I thought I would come in today. I didn't have anything else to do." April leaned against the door frame, blocking Brandon's path back into his office.

"What about your husband? Does he mind your working on Saturday?"

"Martin? No. We don't live together anymore. He drank too much, and I just wasn't going to put up with that. I might have put up with another woman. At least then, he would have been *really* nice to me. The liquor, however, made him mean and ugly." April smiled. "What about your wife? Doesn't she mind your working on Saturday?"

"What?" Brandon was so startled by her boldness he couldn't respond.

"Your wife. What's her name? Claire? Doesn't she mind your being away from home on the weekends?"

Brandon was ruffled and afraid it showed. Even though April hadn't accused him of avoiding Claire, she was too close to the truth. "She knows how much work it takes to keep an operation like this going. She supports me in whatever I have to do."

April thought his response sounded as phony as the computer calls telling you you've won a sweepstakes. Her prey was in her crosshairs. *Focus*, she reminded herself. Pull back the trigger and slowly release it.

"That's wonderful!" April shifted her weight like she was going to head back to her office. Brandon moved forward to go into his office, but April halted, and they collided. Pretending to fall, April grabbed Brandon by the waist pulling him toward her. Gravity became her partner as they fell backward onto the rug. With Brandon on top of her, April continued to hold onto him. He didn't resist. Neither one of them moved for a few seconds. Then April began to moan. Quickly brought back to reality, Brandon jumped up. April stayed on the floor.

"Are you all right?"

April didn't answer him at first. When he dropped down to one knee and shook her gently, she stirred. "Can you help me up?"

"Of course!"

"Help me onto the couch, please. I'm a little woozy." April leaned into Brandon as he practically lifted her off the floor and into a standing position in one movement. He lowered her onto the couch and sat down beside her with his arm around her.

"I am so sorry," he said. "I wasn't watching where I was going."

"No harm, no foul. But, I may have to think twice about working on Saturdays unless I'm covered by workmen's compensation when I'm off the clock!"

Brandon frowned.

"I'm just kidding, Brandon!" April knew he wouldn't object to her calling him Brandon. After thinking he nearly killed her, it would make him appear less than chivalrous to object.

"Oh!" he laughed. He noticed her calling him by his first name, but he didn't mind. It actually felt pretty good. All the women he knew worked for him, and they all called him Mr. Foster. Brandon's arm was still around April. He liked it, and she wasn't objecting.

April was acutely aware of every nuance of this scene. She casually put her hand on his knee and then used it to support herself as she tried to rise from the couch. Feigning weakness, she plopped down on the cushions, allowing her hand to drift toward his upper leg.

"Maybe I better sit still for a minute. I'm still a little dizzy. I guess I hit the floor pretty hard! It's not every day a big guy like you falls on me!" said April with a soft chuckle. Brandon laughed. He felt good, better than he'd felt in a long time.

April was a master of manipulation, and she knew better than to let him drink from the well too long. She eased to the edge of the cushion and stood up. Heading for the office door with Brandon following her, she turned and placed her hand on his cheek briefly. Too quick for him to respond, but too long for it to be an accident. Then she left his office.

Bull's-eye! April thought. She had taken her first big step toward the kind of power she craved. Caution would have to be her watchword if she wanted to reel him in.

Three weeks later April received a call from one of the people she had labeled "Movers and Shakers." These were all men who owned their own companies or were top management. A section in her Rolodex under the heading of M&S listed the names of these men. Another card labeled C&C stood for "Cuddle and Curry." Both were men and women who could be useful to her. April knew how to curry favor in a lot of ways. Some of the tactics worked on both men and women, but cuddling was something she preferred to restrict to men — not that she would go so far as to *limit* it to men if the reward was worth it.

"Well, young lady, I don't believe I recognize your voice. You sound awful sweet, though. Have we met?"

April immediately slipped into her Southern belle routine, drawing out her vowels, but not too far. Going overboard was an invitation for disaster, and it was better to only use the drawl when being coy was expected. If she could have made herself blush on command, that too would have been part of her repertoire. Unfortunately, she just couldn't pull it off. So she settled for the drawl and the Southern belle gestures.

"Well, sir, I don't believe we have. I'm sure I would have remembered such a mellifluous voice as yours! So you are…?" she asked, leaving the caller panting to answer her question.

Clearing his throat, apparently to make sure the honeyed tones were not impeded in any way, he replied, "My name is Chad Winston. I'm a good friend of Brandon's. We go wa-a-ay back."

April knew Brandon had only been in the city for three years. So either Chad was lying, or he was a farm boy originally himself. "Are you saying you are a farmer, Mr. Winston?"

"Huh? Oh, no, and call me Chad, darling. I'm no farmer. I'm a city boy. I met Brandon the first day he moved into the city. We just hit it off and have been friends ever since!"

Not wanting to give Chad too much personal time, April returned to her professional persona. "So, what can I do for you today, Mr. Winston?"

"Uh-unh-unh!" he chided.

"Oh! I'm sorry—Chad. Would you like to speak with Mr. Foster?" April bit the inside of her cheek to keep from laughing.

"Yeah, honey. I've got something important to tell him. You married, hon?"

The last question even caught April off guard. Some guys worked *very* fast. "Not for all practical purposes," she replied.

He laughed. "I think I'm gonna like you!"

Without replying, she put the call on hold to buzz Brandon's office. He picked up immediately. "Yes?"

"Mr. Foster, Mr. Winston is on line one. He says he has something very important to tell you."

"Thank you." Brandon was still unnerved by their Saturday encounter several weekends ago. Fighting his impulses, he had managed to keep walls between them, making sure he didn't come into the office on Saturdays or Sundays. So far it was working. Pushing down the button for line one, he said, "Hello, you old coot! What's up?"

"Who are you calling an old coot? You're older than I am!" Pushing aside the banter, Chad asked, "Remember the rumor you mentioned about a large contractor out of Atlanta being in town?"

Knowing Chad's need to always release his news in a covert way, Brandon played along. "Yeah. So?"

"They tell me listening to the rumor mill can be very lucrative. Of course I never pay any attention to rumors myself, but when you mentioned you heard a rumor that this large contractor ... what was the name? Dietz and Holcombe? That's right. Dietz and Holcombe ... that they were looking for a thousand acres of prime property for an upscale apartment project, I just wondered if you were planning to investigate. I've heard they're going to move on to Dallas this weekend if they don't find what they're looking for here this week."

Brandon responded as Chad expected. "It's good you called because I've been wavering about whether to check out the rumor. I just started trying to get some background information on them. I sure as hell don't want to waste my time making a proposal to a small time contractor. I mean a thousand acres would require some hefty financing for them."

"Isn't this the same company Bill Schmidt was talking about at the club the other night? If he's dealt with them, they've got to be legit. You know how anal he is!" remarked Chad. "Well, none of my business really. I just don't want you to miss an opportunity to make more money, which reminds me about why I really called. It's time for us to review your investments. Things can change fast, and I don't want you to be caught with your pants down when the bell rings!" Chad laughed at his own joke.

"I planned to call you today anyway. If I do decide to make a proposal, I'll have to make sure all my ducks are in a row when they start checking me out."

"Great! Listen. I'm booked all day. Would it be too inconvenient to make a dinner meeting out of it?"

"That'd be perfect, Chad. It gives me time to finish up some things here."

"I'll pick you up at the office at four-thirty. I'm in the mood for ribs. How about you?"

"What do you think?" Brandon asked, laughing as Chad hung up and he pressed down the switch hook. Seeing the slight delay before the light went out on the phone line, he hesitated. *No, it must be his imagination,* he thought and shook his head. April quickly replaced the receiver and got busy with paperwork.

While Brandon and Chad were eating ribs and planning to take the world by storm, April had her own plans. Pulling out her Rolodex, she started calling hotels in the area. She was sure the men from Dietz and Holcombe would be staying within ten miles of the airport because most of the major land investment companies were not located in the downtown area. Their offices were located closer to the areas of growth. After nine calls, she found them. Glancing at her watch, she knew she had just enough time to freshen up and change into a dress which accentuated her assets before the bar at the Hilton started to fill up. She was placing her bet that these guys would be ready for a drink after meeting with hungry prospects all day.

Forty-five minutes later April walked to the door of the bar and stopped, posing herself seductively. The backlight of the lobby lights added a dreamlike quality to the vision for anyone watching, and April was counting on people watching. She had managed to get the names of the two men representing Dietz and Holcombe: Jeffrey Taber and Mark Wagner. So zeroing in on them would not be as difficult as it might have been. Plus, the bar wasn't that crowded yet. She'd be able to eliminate quite a few targets before the rush began. Twenty minutes later, April knew everyone in the bar and none of them were with Dietz and Holcombe.

Her amazing ability to pull everyone around her into her world was classified as awesome by Joe Public, but medical professionals classified it as the byproduct of her disorder. Although diagnosed long ago as bipolar, or manic-depressive as it was once called, April saw it as a blessing. What the doctors called her "manic phases," she considered a special gift. No one else she knew could be as magnetic as she could. Oh, she knew her doctors had said the shift from manic to depressed was out of her control, but she didn't agree. She knew what she was doing every minute.

Her circle of friends continued to grow. Then she noticed a man standing in the doorway, watching the crowd of people in the bar. A little ripple of excitement passed through April. Jumping up, she ran to the door.

"Hey! Don't hang out in the doorway. Come on in and join us," she said, taking him by the arm and guiding him toward the bar. "Everybody! This is ..." She paused, waiting for him to fill in the blank.

"Jeffrey," he said.

"Jeffrey!" she announced so everyone could hear. The patrons all clapped. Getting into the spirit of things, Jeffrey took a bow. The crowd returned to their group gabfest as April, slipping onto a barstool, motioned for Jeffrey to join her.

"Is there some kind of celebration going on here?" Jeffrey asked.

"Celebration?" She looked quizzical. "Oh!" she laughed. "You mean because everyone seems to know each other?" He nodded. "No," she replied, smiling sweetly. "I just seem to have this knack for drawing people together."

He looked around at what looked more like a class reunion than a group of strangers in a bar. "Yeah, I think you could say that."

"What are you doing here in town? Or do you live here?" She added, "I mean, I live here, but I'm still sitting in a hotel bar."

"Actually I'm staying here. I just got finished with one hellacious day of meetings." He shook his head as if trying to clear his mind of the memories.

"Bad news?" she asked.

"It's not important," he replied.

Trying another tack, she asked, "What do you do, Jeffrey? I'd say you look like a stock broker or something, but there's something about you that's a little more grounded than the stock brokers I know." Before he could answer, she said, "Hmmm, let me see," stroking her chin with her thumb and index finger. "You look more like a guy who deals with the real world — maybe construction."

He grinned. "Have you ever looked into fortune-telling as a career?"

"You mean I'm right?" she asked, pretending surprise.

"Pretty damn close. I'm CEO of Dietz and Holcombe, a company out of Chicago. We buy land and develop it."

"You mean houses?"

"Sometimes. We also build apartments or commercial buildings, whatever kind of project we believe will be an asset to a community."

"So what are you doing here?" she asked.

He sighed. "Well, we have this project we wanted to develop here. It's an apartment project but not like anything you've ever seen before." He grimaced as he thought about all the land he'd seen in the last week and how none of it was suitable for the apartment and retail community they had in mind. "Anyway, we've run out of possibilities. Mark — he's my partner on this trip — and I decided to cut our losses and move on to Dallas tomorrow evening."

Priming herself now that the moment had arrived, April looked appropriately distraught over his difficulties. "What exactly are you looking for?"

Jeffrey looked at her strangely, wondering why she would even want to know. Still, he thought, no harm in answering. "At least a thousand acres with the potential for expansion. It needs to be in an area that's considered in the path of growth for the city. We don't want to invest this much money in an area that's dying. Refurbishing is not what this project is about. We want to add value to an already promising community."

"You mean you couldn't find anything?" she asked in surprise.

"Everything we've been shown just doesn't meet the criteria." He wondered why he was talking to this strange woman about his business, but again decided it couldn't cause any damage. Besides, letting off steam was probably a good thing — clear the air before heading for Dallas to start all over again.

Thoughtfully, April bit on her bottom lip. "I just may be able to help you."

Jeffrey choked slightly on his drink. "What?!" he asked. "*Who* are you?"

Smiling back at him, she said, "I may be the answer to your problem. What would you say if I told you I know where you can get your hands on a 1200 acre parcel that's not only in the path of growth, but is next to a high-end residential community?"

"What's the matter with it? Toxic waste dump? Floodplain?"

April laughed. "Now, don't be negative," she chided. "I just happen to work for a man who owns a land investment and construction company. I guess that's why I recognized the signs in you—"

"Signs?" he asked.

"Yeah, the signs telling me you definitely weren't a stock broker."

"Oh," he said, setting his glass down on the bar.

"Anyway, if you're game," she said, glancing around the room and then at her watch, "uh, I can set up a meeting with him for you." She didn't want him to think it mattered that much to her. Bringing her gaze back to him, she asked, "Are you going to be in town long enough?"

"Well, we have reservations for 6:30 pm tomorrow night."

"That's plenty of time. Well, are you interested?" she asked, glancing again at her watch.

"Sure. What's your boss' name?"

"Mr. Foster. Brandon Foster. He owns BFI, which is Brandon Foster Investments. Most people just call it BFI. Have you heard of it?"

He hesitated. "No, I don't think I have. It sounds vaguely familiar, but it may just be the acronym that's familiar. Isn't there a waste management company with those initials?"

She laughed. "Yeah. We build, and they take out the trash."

Jeffrey chuckled. "Okay, how can I get in touch with you or Mr. Foster?"

"Wait a minute. I know he went to dinner with an old friend. Maybe I can reach him on his pager." She pulled out her address book and pulled the bar phone toward her. After dialing the number, she waited and then tapped in the phone number at the bar. She hoped he would call quickly—out of curiosity if nothing else. Her prayer was answered when the phone jangled within less than a minute.

"Hello?" she said, picking up the receiver before the bartender beat her to it.

Sounding confused, Brandon said, "April?" although he had recognized her voice immediately.

"Mr. Foster! I'm so glad you returned my page. I have a gentleman here with Dietz & Holcombe – a Mr. Jeffrey – "She looked inquiringly at Jeffrey, not wanting to divulge she already knew his last name.

"Taber," he whispered.

"Taber," she continued. "He's the CEO by the way. Anyway, he's interested in looking at the 1200 acre parcel you own out east." Before Brandon could reply, she continued, "There's just one catch. He's got a 6:30 flight tomorrow night. So if you want to meet with him, it will have to be in the morning. Will this work for you?"

Flabbergasted by the turn of events, all Brandon could do was stammer out an "A-Absolutely!"

"Fine! I'll take care of the arrangements, and we will see you at the office in the morning. Have a great evening!" she declared before hanging up.

Standing there with the phone receiver in his hand, Brandon looked as disoriented as a man who'd just stepped out onto the sidewalk after being hopelessly caught in a revolving door for the last three minutes. Chad walked over. "What's up guy? You look freaked."

"No, not freaked exactly, more like blown away."

"Who was that?"

"April."

"The receptionist April?" Brandon nodded. "What the hell did she want?"

"You're not going to believe this, but she's set up a meeting for me with the CEO of Dietz & Holcombe tomorrow to look at those 1200 acres!"

"Damn! How'd she do that?" Chad asked, impressed.

"Beats me, but the office gossip mill seems to think she has her fingers in everything, at least according to Rhonda and Norman. I never paid it any attention, but apparently there is some truth to the rumor."

"Well at least she seems to be on your side," remarked Chad, slapping Brandon on the back before heading back toward the table.

Chapter 4

Jeffrey Taber

After hooking Brandon up with Jeffrey Taber and the deal closed, April worked both sides of the duo to manipulate them into letting her be the liaison between BFI and Dietz and Holcombe. As a result, she spent more time than necessary traveling to Chicago. While there, she played Jeffrey like the proverbial fiddle. It took nearly nine months for her to get all the pieces in place, including ridding herself of her husband Martin, but finally she was ready.

On her monthly trip to Chicago, April called Jeffrey from the hotel limousine. "Jeffrey, darling," she said when he answered the phone.

"April? I wasn't expecting you until Wednesday."

"I know, Jeffrey, but something has come up I thought you should know about, and I didn't want to talk about it over the phone." She struggled to sound distressed, but the excitement of the hunt was making it difficult.

"What is it? Is something wrong on the job?" Jeffrey sat up straight in his desk chair. They were too far into the project to turn back.

Hoping to increase the tension, she answered, "Yes, but I think we can fix it."

"What?! What is it?" Jeffrey rose from his chair along with his heightened tension.

"Look. I'll be at the hotel in five minutes. I'll drop off my luggage and head straight over to the office. I'll be there in less than thirty minutes," she said, "and Jeffrey, whatever you do, don't call the Memphis office. Okay?" Her voice sounded strained.

Hesitating, Jeffrey said, "Okay, but hurry."

Smiling, April hung up the phone. Things were coming together nicely.

Stepping out of the taxi she had grabbed outside the hotel, April straightened her dress before closing the passenger door, took a deep breath, and formed her face into a worried façade before turning toward the office building. A fortunate choice as it turned out because Jeffrey came rushing through the double doors from the lobby toward her.

"Jeffrey! You startled me," she cried, placing her hand on her chest, only partly for effect.

"Well, you've got me all worked up yourself! What the hell's going on?" Jeffrey demanded as he took her arm, practically dragging her down the sidewalk.

"Where are we going?" she gasped. Doubt started to creep into her mind about whether she had miscalculated.

"I don't want to be in the office in case I need to kill you," he replied.

"What?!" she cried out, stopping dead in her tracks despite his forward momentum nearly pulling her arm out of its socket.

"I was just kidding. Surely you know the old saying about killing the messenger bearing bad news?" he said.

Not liking the analogy at all but careful not to show it, she laughed. "There for a minute you scared me, but if it's safer, I'll just hurry down to the Western Union office and send you a telegram instead."

Jeffrey chuckled. "Okay, I'll back off," he said, releasing her arm, "but let's step into this bistro and find a corner table. I think I need a Turkish coffee, no sugar."

Walking toward a table, April said, "I think I'll have an Irish coffee. If you're going to kill me, I may as well get a little tipsy."

"Perhaps mud coffee *is* a little extreme. I think I'll just settle for coffee black," he said pushing her chair forward as she sat down. He waved at the waiter as he walked around the table to his chair. Ordering for them both, he leaned back in his chair. "Okay, tell me."

"Well, I was working at the office this weekend. I was alone. I've had some suspicions something was going on. Nothing concrete you know, just hushed tones or conversations stopping when I walked in—

all things that could just be personal issues, but it has been bugging me. So I acted like I was going to be out of town this weekend. Instead, I went into the office to look through the files in Brandon's office—"

"How did you get access to them? Doesn't he lock his office? I know I do."

"Sure he does, but I still have a key from a long time ago — before you came into the picture. He probably doesn't realize I even have it." April knew Brandon was not aware she had duplicated his key within weeks of being hired. It had been so simple. Back then Brandon was trusting enough to leave his office unlocked with the key in his desk except at night, and if you're the only one in the office while everyone else is at lunch — well, it was a piece of cake.

"Anyway, I went into his office and looked through the files. That's when I found it."

"Found what?" Jeffrey was trying to restrain his urge to shout at her.

"The plans for ripping you off for millions," she said quietly, glancing over her shoulder as if she expected Brandon to suddenly appear in the bistro.

"What the hell? Are you sure you know what you're talking about?" Jeffrey's head was spinning. This was not just a big project for him. It was the bellwether for a new trend Dietz & Holcombe was hoping would make it the frontrunner in the construction industry across the country. A lot was riding on its success—money, reputation, his job.

"Well, I may not be an accountant, but when I find a document listing the names of phony suppliers with amounts set up for each month starting after the first year's audit all the way through the end of the project, I think even I can add two and two and come up with four!" she declared, involuntarily allowing her anger to show. To counter the acerbic tone of her remark, she scooted her chair closer to him.

"I'm sorry. I didn't mean—" Jeffrey said.

"That's okay. I'm sorry, too. I didn't mean to be so hateful. I'm just so upset about all this. I've been worrying about it all weekend. I feel responsible. After all, I was the one who introduced the two of you." April wiped at imaginary tears.

Scooting toward her, he put his arm around her shoulder. "It's not your fault, April. If it weren't for your ethics, I might not ever have found out about this."

April lowered her face into her hands and snuffled. She held her eyes tightly closed and pressed the tips of her fingers against them until she could feel them burning. "What's wrong?" asked Jeffrey.

"Oh, nothing," she replied, raising her head as if nothing was amiss.

"Are you crying?" he asked.

"No. It's just that — well, now there's a good chance I'll be out on the street. I mean Brandon will know I'm the only one who could have told you even if he doesn't know how I found out. I don't really think I'll get a raise, you know?"

Startled that he hadn't given any thought at all to how this was going to affect April, Jeffrey was ashamed. "Listen. Don't worry. I'll make sure you have a job — if not in Memphis, then here in Chicago. It's the least I can do," he said, patting her arm as she let her head rest on his shoulder. Chastising himself, Jeffrey might have felt differently if he could see the smile on April's downcast face.

When their coffees arrived, April and Jeffrey slid their chairs apart, and April got out her compact to freshen her face. Almost restored to her original perfection, April put the compact back into her purse and sipped her Irish coffee before making the announcement she knew would close the deal for her.

"I made copies of the notes," she said, calmly sipping on her coffee as if unaware of the importance of her statement.

"You what? You mean you actually have proof? Did you bring it with you?"

"Well, of course. Why else would you believe me if I didn't have proof?" What she didn't tell him was that she had been carefully working on the so-called notes for the last six months. She had spent night after night practicing Brandon Foster's handwriting and signature. She didn't want to push her luck too far, though. So she had used his typewriter to type most of the notes, just making brief markings on the notes, but enough for his handwriting to be recognizable.

Opening an account in Brandon’s name in an offshore bank was her coup de grâce, her death blow, for with her carefully crafted notes, he was already mortally wounded. Getting the necessary information for the account was simple, and since his presence was not required, she simply copied his passport, filled out the paperwork, signed it, and sent it off. Since all the office mail came to her first, intercepting the return authorizations was no problem. Before leaving Memphis, she had put the documents from the bank and the infamous notes in with Brandon's personal reconciled bank statements because she knew he never looked at them once they were reconciled.

April leaned down to get her briefcase. Pulling out only Xerox copies of the notes, she laid them in front of Jeffrey, saying a silent prayer Brandon didn't decide to rummage through his old bank statements for some reason.

"Where are the originals?" Jeffrey asked after a few minutes.

"In his file cabinet in the folder with his personal bank statements," she replied.

The muscle in Jeffrey's face was twitching. April could see he was battling with himself about how to handle the situation. In truth, Brandon hadn't actually done anything yet. The notes only showed intent. Jeffrey sighed. "This is a sticky situation, April. I can't accuse him of something he hasn't done yet. I mean—well," he said, shaking the notes for emphasis, "it's just a piece of paper."

"Would it make a difference if you knew he had opened an offshore bank account?"

Jeffrey's brow arched. "Has he?"

"Yeah, I also found papers showing he opened it the end of last month. Seems sort of coincidental, don't you think? I mean, the dates on the notes start the month after the first year's audit, which, if I'm not mistaken is the end of this month, and he just happens to open an offshore account right now?" She arches her brow, mirroring him. "By the way, I have copies of that, too."

****

The speed with which Jeffrey dealt with the situation shocked even April. Within one week, he had flown to Memphis with his attorney, forced Brandon off the project as well as forced him to sign an agreement stating he would not contest the decision. Jeffrey had made it quite clear he had plenty of evidence to take him to court and enough money to keep him there until he was ruined. Brandon's protests of innocence fell on deaf ears.

April, of course, acted shocked and dismayed at the turn of events. After Jeffrey and his lawyer left, she found Brandon sitting in his office staring at his desk.

"Is there anything I can do to help, Mr. Foster?" she asked.

"No, April. I don't think anyone can help me right now."

"What happened? I heard Mr. Taber yelling about a bank account and some plans or something. Was something wrong with the building plans or the construction draws?" she asked innocently.

"If you must know, and I'm sure you would eventually anyway, he accused me of planning to embezzle funds from the company. He even had proof of a bank account set up in my name." Looking wistfully at April as if she might offer him a reprieve, he asked, "How could this happen? Who could have done this to me?"

"How could anyone have set up a bank account for you without your knowing it? Maybe your financial advisor would know." The moment the last word fell from her lips, she saw Brandon mentally take aim at Chad Winston. He knew more about him than anyone, *and* he was his financial advisor. "Well, if you need me for anything," she said, wrinkling her brow in false sympathy, "I'll be at my desk."

She left the room, knowing she had just divided and conquered. BFI would dog-paddle or sink, but it would never taste real success again. Brandon had finally lost his spirit, but it was for the greater good — hers.

****

Two years passed, and Brandon Foster had become a faded memory for April. If a fleeting thought of him passed through her mind, she felt a slight fondness because without him, it would have taken longer to get where she was now. Reminiscing or worrying about the past was a waste of time as far as April was concerned, however. The only thing that mattered was the Now, and how the Now would affect her future. Three years ago there was no past to waste time on — only the Now and the future, and she had gone after it with her claws carefully concealed until she was in striking distance. Then she'd made a clean cut without a drop of blood splashing in her direction.

Chicago was her kind of town. Unlike Memphis, which still held on to its country ways, Chicago didn't even try to conceal its rapacious nature. Oh, there were calculated dance steps that mimicked civility, but everyone who was in the game knew that once the clock struck midnight and the dance was over, their true natures could be revealed. April loved it. Living in this town was like being at University, and working for Dietz & Holcombe was like taking on an internship.

Behind closed doors, there were no punches pulled and no pretense related to the outside world. Of course, they still danced among themselves for in the world of Dietz & Holcombe, getting to the upper rungs carried great rewards. The Memphis project, which had been christened the Village Project, had started a trend across the country, and Jeffrey Taber was leading the charge to the tune of billions. Not surprisingly, April was carefully polishing his sword, literally and figuratively.

"April, can you come into my office? I want to discuss something with you," asked Jeffrey over the intercom.

April had her chair turned around and was looking out at the view from her penthouse office, the perk of being a vice-president. Gazing out over the city from here, she felt the power of it all surging through her veins. Hearing Jeffrey's voice over the intercom at that moment added an extra kick. She smiled. What could have been better? Not only was she able to get to the top of the heap without so much as a stumble, the one she rode to get there was quite extraordinary in bed. Of course, April was not one to love another unless there was something more than sexual benefits. Even then, love had never found a crack wide enough to seep into her soul. Still, if sex was part of the program, it was a bonus if it was actually satisfying.

"Yes, Jeffrey. I'll be right there." April went into her bathroom to touch up her makeup. It was good policy to always look your best.

Stepping inside his office a few minutes later, she closed the door behind her. "What's the problem, Jeffrey?" she asked, taking a seat in front of his desk.

"No problem. I just wondered if you know anything about Harmon Industries."

"Hmmm. Harmon Industries. No, I don't think so. Why?" she asked.

"It's an outfit out of California. I've heard them mentioned at the Club, but nothing specific — at least nothing I can remember."

"Then why are you asking about them?" April's antennae were up. Any threat to Jeffrey or Dietz & Holcombe was a personal threat.

"I'm not really sure, but I've heard they may be bidding against us for a piece of property in Minnesota."

"Are you saying they want the property for a different kind of project?" If this was the case, April wasn't worried. Land was land after all, and there was only so much of it. It was only natural to come up against opposition.

"No, the rumor is that they want the land for a Village Project of their own."

"What!?" April stood up. "You mean they've come all the way from California to bid against us for a competitive project? Why don't they just go somewhere else and build their own?"

"This is why I'm concerned. There are smaller companies copying our basic designs all over the country, but this is the first time one of them has tried to throw us out of the sandbox." Jeffrey swiveled his chair around to look out the window. April knew that view held the same rejuvenating sense of power for him as it did for her. She waited.

Turning back to face her, he said, "April, we need to find out as much as we can about this company and the men behind it. I don't know anyone better able to ferret out this kind of information than you." He grinned at her.

Pretending to be embarrassed by his praise, she dropped her head before raising her eyes to coyly meet his. He guffawed. "That might work on someone else, but I didn't get off a turnip truck this morning."

"Oh, kind sir, whatever are you talking about?" she teased.

Laughing, he said, "Get out of here before I lose all restraint."

Giving a small curtsy, she left the room with one quick glance over her shoulder. He was watching her every movement. He waved his hand in dismissal just as the phone rang. Smiling, he picked up the receiver.

"Jeffrey, it's me. Are you going to make it home in time for dinner at the Benson's tonight?" his wife asked.

"Of course, sweetheart. Didn't I promise you?"

"I know, but sometimes things happen—"

"You know—"

"I know it's not your fault, darling. I just wanted to know if I need to make arrangements for getting there on my own."

Relaxing, he said, "No, nothing is going to interfere. I'm looking forward to spending time with old friends. I've had enough business dinners lately."

"Great! See you soon, darling," she replied and hung up.

****

The Bensons lived in an old mansion that brought forth memories of the wealthy lifestyles of the great industrialists earlier in the century. It was three stories tall with a grand circular driveway leading to the front steps. Once there, a valet opened your doors and drove your car away into its own luxurious quarters while another member of the Bensons' staff escorted you into the grand manor. You were announced to any who might be listening and then allowed to wander on your own.

As the Tabers waylaid the nearest waiter and grabbed two glasses of champagne, Jeffrey remarked, "Reckon we'll actually see the Bensons tonight?"

Laughing, Elisa said, "I hope so, but it looks like it's not their usual dinner party. I see a lot of people here I haven't laid eyes on in a long time. Look! There's Marion Westpenny. I haven't seen her in at least two years! Darling, can you manage on your own? I just have to catch up with her."

Sighing, Jeffrey pretended it would be a strain, but he would try to manage. Punching him on the shoulder, Elisa said, "If I need you, I'll just search the bars." Playfully, he stuck his tongue out at her. Watching her walk away, he was reminded of how much he loved her. Thoughts of April intruded, but they didn't cause a ripple in the ocean of feelings he felt for Elisa. April was only a diversion, a chance to walk on the edge, to briefly be someone other than the person he knew himself to be. Elisa was his soul mate, and April — well, he knew April was using him as much as he was using her.

Across the huge ballroom Elisa caught up with Marion Westpenny and hugged her tightly. "Girl, I have missed seeing you! What have you been up to?"

"Not much and everything! You know how it is. You just try to stay on track until you realize that the train's not going anywhere so you change trains."

Laughing, Elisa said, "You are the world's worst at underselling yourself, Marion! Seriously, what's going on in your life?"

"Better question: what's going on in yours?" Marion asked, frowning slightly.

Startled, but deciding she misread her friend, Elisa replied, "Well, Jeffrey works and makes lots of money, and I spend hours thinking of new ways to spend it."

"No, really," Marion inquired.

"What are you talking about?" Elisa asked, her heart thumping a little too hard.

Taking her elbow, Marion led Elisa into a small side parlor, which incredibly no one had yet discovered. "I've been hearing for the last year about what's been going on, but I didn't want to believe it. I should have gotten in touch with you earlier, but I guess I'm a coward."

"What the hell are you talking about, Marion?"

Marion's mouth dropped open. "I can't believe this! I would never … I thought … I'm so sorry!" she said as she hugged Elisa.

Pushing her away, Elisa demanded, "I said, what are you talking about?"

Visibly shaken, Marion clamped her lips together as if any more words escaping from them would tear hers and Elisa's worlds asunder. Elisa gave her no quarter, staring boldly into her eyes and refusing to shift her gaze. Marion would never intentionally hurt her friend, but the rumors — she'd thought they were facts, not rumors — oh, God! Nothing to do but plunge in.

"Elisa, I wish it wasn't me telling you this, but I really thought it was out in the open. I just thought you were trying to hide your feelings in front of everyone—"

"Marion, if you don't stop dilly-dallying, I'm going to scream!"

"Everyone says Jeffrey is having an affair with that woman in his office — you know, the one who moved up here from Memphis."

Elisa didn't make a sound. She simply hugged Marion and walked away, leaving her friend to wonder if she would ever talk to her again. Looking around the ballroom, Elisa spotted her husband leaning on the bar talking to Henry Benson. Jeffrey was so handsome. Even though he was closing in quickly on forty, he was lean and hard. His hair was a dark chocolate color and so thick he had to have it cut and styled regularly to keep it under control. Looking at him now, she didn't want to believe what Marion had told her, but she knew she was a fool if she thought other women wouldn't make a play for him. She just never thought — well, she had always thought they had something special. She *knew* they had something special.

Shaking her head, she warned herself not to jump to conclusions. Walking across the room and sliding her arm through his, she whispered, "Do you mind if we call it a night?"

Puzzled but hopeful, Jeffrey replied, "No, I'd rather spend it alone with you anyway."

Pouring a drink for himself and Elisa, Jeffrey sensed that whatever was wrong was not going to be easily resolved. He had never known his wife to be this reticent about expressing herself. She had ridden home in silence, unwilling or unable to laugh at his jokes. That was when his hopes about a romantic evening were quashed. Now he was just waiting for the explosion because he could already feel the cautionary tremors.

Finally she spoke. "What's the name of that woman in your office? You know, the one from Memphis?"

Trying not to let his terror show on his face, Jeffrey calmly answered, "Oh, you mean April Saunders?"

"Yes, April Saunders. How long have you been sleeping with her?"

Chapter 5

The view from her high rise apartment did little to cheer April. From her sofa she watched Lake Michigan. Although there was nothing between her and the lake to warn of the wind, she could tell from the surface waves, roiling toward shore, that the wind was up. She watched as the waves crashed on the shore, losing their power. She felt their defeat every time the water crashed near shore — white foam billowing up in one last climactic performance before dissipating into trickles of water racing to return to the way it was before being stopped by the power of the sand.

It had been two months since the debacle at Dietz & Holcombe, but April was still suffering from mild shock. Her usual euphoric state of mind was having difficulty maintaining control against Jeffrey's unjust actions. What the hell was his problem? He could have just denied the affair to his wife, and everything could have continued as it was, except, of course, for their affair. April didn't care about that part at all. It certainly wasn't an *affaire de coeur*. Besides, she would never give her heart to anyone weak enough to be manipulated by her.

Taking a drag on the cigarette which had nearly burned up in the ashtray, April let her gaze touch once more on the trickles of water on shore, racing back toward the lake. "That isn't me!" she declared to the wind, the water, and the sand. Her familiar air of determination returned, lifting her spirits. There was no way someone like Jeffrey Taber would get the best of her. Grabbing the paper, she began searching for job listings in the *Tribune*.

The severance package from Dietz & Holcombe had been generous, a fact she was quite sure Elisa Taber knew nothing about so she wasn't pushed to find a job right away. Coupled with her savings, she had enough to support herself in the style she deserved for at least three years. She didn't want to wait that long to get back in the game, however. She realized everything up to now had simply been a dress rehearsal. From now on, everything she did would be geared toward experiencing ever-intensifying triumphs in her life. There would be no more fading away for her.

Still, things had not gone as well as April had hoped. Every morning like clockwork, she'd read the want ads in the paper from one end to the other, and no jobs had leaped into her lap. After the first two weeks, she'd stopped skipping over the clerical jobs. After a month, her resolve wavering, she considered being a truck driver. After all, she could go to truck drivers' school and still get a job well before her money ran out. Then she thought about the long hours alone with nothing but the endless ramblings of other drivers and the lewd remarks that were sure to come. She had quit reading those ads. Actually, clerical jobs or retail jobs were about the only things for which she could qualify. No one seemed to care she had been vice-president of a large construction company. Of course, there was always the problem of references. Brandon definitely wasn't going to help her case, and despite Jeffrey's generous severance, he probably wouldn't either.

April refused to believe her dreams could end so abruptly before they hardly took form. The timing was off — that was all. When another two weeks dragged by with no prospects on the horizon, she changed her approach. Not every golden opportunity had to start at the top, she decided. Look at the job she'd had when working for Brandon Foster. She was a receptionist for cripes' sake, and look where that led! Well, perhaps it hadn't ended so well, what with later being fired by Jeffrey and all, but she had made it to the top. Next time she would just be more careful. Bottom line: she would start looking at the kind of companies hiring receptionists and secretaries rather than worrying about the job itself. All she needed was a foot in the door.

Chapter 6

Nora Oliver

The warmth of the sun on April's back as she walked down the sidewalk was like a warm hand, nudging her forward into her dreams. She really felt good about this interview. The job was as a secretary/receptionist for a small publishing house called Oliver & Company. She had already spoken briefly with Nora Oliver on the phone. She sounded like April's mother had — comfortable with herself, her voice a little sultry, which always sounded strange to April coming from an older woman. Based on their conversation, April was certain the interview was just a formality.

Rounding the corner, she saw the sign for Oliver & Company on the front of the building across the street. The brass letters looked very majestic against the old, red brick — almost like they had always been there. She quickly crossed the street. She took a deep breath, pulled her shoulders back, and walked through the front door with the confident air that had worked for her before and she knew would work for her again.

"Well, April," said Mrs. Oliver, directing her to a chair across from her desk. "You don't mind if I call you April, do you?" Smiling brightly, April shook her head, noticing the woman wasn't as old as she had assumed. "I thoroughly enjoyed my chat with you on the phone, but I have to say I am puzzled by your resume."

"Puzzled?"

"I suppose that describes it best. First of all, I'm puzzled about your past employment. Apparently your first employer is unreachable, bankrupt I believe, and yet you managed to acquire the position of vice-president in a very prestigious construction firm here in the city. Quite a feat for someone only twenty-eight years old."

"Is that so strange?" asked April, starting to reassess the future of this job.

"Strange? Maybe not, more like unusual. However, my

puzzlement is over your request not to contact your last employer. I managed to confirm you did indeed hold that position with Mr. Jeffrey Taber's company, but I would still like to know why I shouldn't contact him."

Nora Oliver was looking at April the way a mother looked at her daughter when she suspected she was hiding something. April wasn't fooled into thinking Nora was a pushover, however. Still, she was willing to play the role she was being offered if it got her the job.

Dropping her head for a moment, April took a deep breath before replying. "Well, it got rather complicated, if you know what I mean."

"Tell me," Nora said.

"Well," April began, knowing full well that whatever she said, it was not verifiable, "after a while we — Jeffrey and I — well, we got involved. It wasn't really serious, just a fling, but his wife didn't see it that way."

"What happened?"

"Well—" she hesitated. "Well, I got a nice severance package."

To her surprise, Nora Oliver burst out laughing. "At least you didn't go away empty-handed!" April didn't know whether to join in her laughter or wait quietly. She chose to wait.

"So my last puzzlement is this: what the heck are you doing applying for a secretarial position? I have to admit I admire your chutzpah in making it to the top so fast and so young, even if you did fall on your ass, but can you even type?"

Not able to suppress a snicker and feeling more confident now about the direction the interview was taking, April replied, "Of course I can type. Isn't that a prerequisite for women in business along with the ability to brew coffee?"

Nora chuckled. "Well, you probably will have to make coffee around here occasionally, and you'll definitely have to type, but just in case you're wondering, I'm the Publisher around here and plan for it to stay that way."

April frowned. "Excuse me?"

"You obviously have ambition so I'm just setting limits for you.

You can aspire to the position of Editor, even Senior Editor, but don't be eyeballing my job. Oliver & Company is my life. My employees are good to me, and I'm good to them. You'll be the only one who hasn't been with me since the beginning two years. The only reason this position is open is because Ruth developed cancer last year. She died a couple of months back. We just haven't been able to face bringing in anyone new until now. I just want you to understand this is a family, and you're the new addition. It might be tough making a place for yourself, but once you do, you'll always be one of the family."

"Does this mean I got the job?" April asked, not wanting to appear too confident.

"I hope you're not this dense all the time," laughed Nora. Reaching out to shake her hand, she added, "Just kidding! You'll get used to it," obviously referring to her sense of humor. Walking her to the door, Nora said, "You don't need to start until next Monday at 8:30, so you have nearly a week to prepare yourself."

Smiling as she crossed the street, April was admonished by a homeless man holding a placard. "You don't know what's coming. You think you do, but you don't!" His words wiped the smile from her face, but just as quickly, she thought, *That's just what you think! My foot is already in the door.*

****

Taking one last look at herself in the reflective surface of the elevator doors, April smoothed her skirt and stepped out into the reception area of Oliver & Company. A large, rather ornate desk sat impressively in the center of the room, a curved wall as its backdrop. April stood quietly, waiting for someone to respond to the ding of the elevator bell. A short, stocky woman entered through one of the side doorways looking like a cartoon caricature of an editor. Clad in a loose-fitting, brown skirt with a beige blouse and a cardigan tied around her waist, she stuck a pencil over her ear as she stepped forward to greet April.

"You must be the new secretary, April Saunders," she declared as she stuck out her hand. April smiled and shook hands. "I'm Jean Wilson, and this is your desk, which is why there was no one out here to greet you," she laughed.

"Just put your purse in the bottom drawer there," she added as she deftly plucked a key from the middle drawer and handed it to April. "This is the key to lock that drawer so your purse is secure." When April's purse was safely stowed, Jean said, "Let's go introduce you to the rest of the staff."

****

Although working at Oliver & Company had been pleasant enough so far, it only served to affirm for April she could never be satisfied with a job like this. The good life, the power that goes with position, would always cause her to hunger for it until it was once again hers. Manipulating people to get what she wanted and working in the shadows was personally satisfying, but it didn't even come close to the thrill of openly controlling the lives of other people, knowing they had little or no recourse.

Her new position reminded her of when she had started working for Brandon Foster. No one paid any attention to the receptionist, so in the end you were privy to more than anyone else. Of course, this time she would have to be more careful. Even being a vice-president, screwing Jeffrey Taber, her boss, had been a mistake. Men, especially Jeffrey, were even weaker than she'd thought. Imagine, letting his wife dictate to him about his company! At least April had learned a valuable lesson: a powerful position is still vulnerable so you have to protect it at all costs.

One of April's jobs as receptionist was sorting the incoming mail, pulling the manuscript submissions aside, and then determining which manuscripts had been requested and which were unsolicited. Because Oliver & Company was a small press, they worked directly with authors as much as they worked through agents, so receiving unsolicited manuscripts was commonplace.

After the first week, April approached Jean about the unsolicited manuscripts stacked against the wall behind her desk. She had spot-read some of them. Some were horrendous, but others were pretty good. She was already trying to figure out how she could use them to her advantage. Regardless, she couldn't keep stacking them against the wall because eventually she was going to run out of wall.

"How do you feel about doing more than sorting the manuscripts?" Jean asked. She explained that Ruth had been wonderful at keeping the slush pile from piling up in the editors' offices. She would speed read the first five or six chapters of a manuscript and determine if it had potential or was just amateurish trash. Then she sorted those with potential according to the different editors' areas of interests. This way, an editor knew that if they did resort to the slush pile in the floor in the corner of their office, it was more likely to be fruitful for them.

"Do you think you could try to fill her shoes in this area?" Jean asked. "I know Nora didn't talk to you about this at your interview. I guess she assumed you like to read if you were wanting to work at a publishing house. Do you read fast?"

April had never timed her reading speed so she wasn't really sure. "Well," she said, "it's not unusual for me to read a novel in a single day. I can also read lengthy and complex contracts in a short period of time, but I've never timed myself."

Jean laughed. "I think you'll pass. How do you feel about working with the manuscripts the way Ruth did in addition to your regular duties?"

April's devious mind was already beginning to see the light, illuminating her path to power. In an acquiescent tone, she replied, "I think it would help keep the job from becoming monotonous."

"Great! I'll get you a list of the areas of interest for each editor. Just remember when you're reading the manuscripts that sometimes the story has great potential even if the writer seems to have skipped English class all through school. If the story is good enough, and the writing style is good, we can work with the lack of grammatical or spelling skills. Obviously, these don't float right to the top of the slush pile, but at least they don't land in the waste basket."

April smiled at Jean, but her mind was busy calculating how the manuscripts could be her ticket to the position of power she craved.

Chapter 7

Nine months later...

Struggling with her feelings, April propped her feet up on the ottoman. She was coming out of a depressive phase. She had been fortunate with her mood swings over the last ten years not being as extreme in expression or as often in occurrence as the doctors had first expected. They had eventually diagnosed her as cyclothymic, a mild form of bipolar disorder. The manic and depressive phases could still be disruptive, but they had usually been manageable, especially since she seemed to experience more manic than depressive episodes. There were pluses and minuses to being manic. The increased drive to perform, the extreme optimism, and risky behavior were all attitudes that often pushed her ahead of the pack. The increased sex drive and unwise financial choices which were also symptoms of mania, however, could undo all the benefits if she wasn't careful.

It was a holiday weekend, and April had been sitting on the sofa for nearly the entire weekend. She dreaded going back to the routine at work on Tuesday. She had hardly slept since Thursday. She ordered a pizza on Saturday, thinking something spicy would jumpstart her appetite, but no luck. One piece was all she could stomach. Twenty-four hours later, it was still sitting on the coffee table. The more she thought about still being in a secretarial position under Nora Oliver, the more irritated she became. Something was going to have to give, she thought as she tossed her house shoe across the room.

The next morning April woke to the sun streaming in through the windows. Taking a deep breath, she literally felt a lightness of spirit compared to yesterday. *Thank, God!* Slipping out of bed, she stood up, extended her arms in front of her and touched her toes several times. Grabbing her robe from the bed post, she headed for the kitchen. "Coffee, then I take over the world," she declared.

April had never doubted that the unsolicited manuscripts pouring into the office were going to be her ticket, but she never dreamed it was going to be so much work! Over the last nine months, she had been bringing the better manuscripts home with her. If the story was good and needed very little editing or none at all, she kept the manuscript at her home office. Those with good storylines but needing serious substantive editing, she worked on to glean the outlines of the stories, change all the characters' names and the locations, and create file cards for each one. She had a record system set up that reminded her of the card catalogue in her high school library. Each file card contained a solid story idea with no identifying elements which could link it to any of the manuscripts. These were the manuscripts she returned to the office slush pile.

She had enough inventory now to start thinking about how all this work was going to take her where she wanted to go. She had never doubted that she would either be moving up by unseating Nora or moving out to form her own small press. Well, maybe not small. Doing things in a small way wasn't her style. So what would it be? Taking over Oliver & Company would be sweet, but she realized it wouldn't be nearly as sweet as forming her own company and taking away all Nora's clients, at least the essential ones.

April wasn't seeking retribution against Nora. Actually Nora had been very supportive of her since she was hired. On more than one occasion, Nora had remarked that April was on the fast track to becoming an editor. Nora had taken notice of her about six months earlier when she had been swamped by manuscripts while having to endure an audit. Having already dumped all she could on her other editors, she bit the bullet and asked April to read through a manuscript she had promised to assess by the end of the week for an old friend. Of course, Nora’s promise had been before she knew about the audit. Under ordinary circumstances she would never even have considered letting a secretary read a manuscript for her, but she was desperate.

April assured her she would read it and make notes about anything that she as a reader found troublesome. Of course, Nora didn't know April was already three months into creating her own personal library and had learned a great deal about isolating the theme of a novel and determining if the plot held together. Nora's request was perfect timing! The closer April could get to Nora, the quicker she would know exactly how to taste the sweetness of power again. She worked nonstop on the manuscript and presented Nora not only with observations, but also with suggestions. Nora was so impressed she had been "testing" April ever since. April didn't mind because it gave her legitimate feedback on her editing, both basic and substantive. Even though Nora didn't know it, she was training her successor in one way or another.

Chapter 8

John Blackridge

April heard the ding and looked up to see a man stepping out of the elevator. He was unfamiliar, but she liked what she saw. Smiling, the man walked confidently toward her desk. April had no doubt his hair was once raven black although it now had an ample helping of white scattered throughout. With the white teeth and smoky-gray eyes, she was sure he must be a model for one of the romance novels they published.

"May I help you?" she asked, smiling in return while visions of him reaching across the desk and letting his fingers slide gently down the curve of her neck to the rise of her breasts assailed her.

"Yes. Would you tell Mrs. Oliver that John Blackridge is here?" His eyes never strayed from hers, leaving April slightly shaken. She wondered if he somehow knew what she was imaging. He grinned seductively, the left corner of his mouth lifting slightly, and April felt a concurrent movement deep within her, and a place which was unfamiliar came to life for a brief moment for a single pulse.

"May I tell her what it is in regard to?" she asked, trying to stay on course and regain her composure.

April saw a quick flash of shock on his face even though he recovered quickly. "I haven't seen you before, but I haven't been into the office in quite a while," he replied. "Anyway, you must be new, or you would know that I am one of Nora's bestselling authors."

Feigning embarrassment, April quickly stood and headed toward Nora's office even though she knew she was out of the office. She just needed the time to figure out her next move. *One of the bestselling authors! What luck!* She rarely met any of the big ticket writers. This might be her only chance to make a connection with him. He could turn out to be instrumental in getting her plan off the ground. Hurrying back toward reception, she realized she wanted to explore more than his potential as a writer and career-maker for her. She bypassed her desk and stood directly in front of John.

"I am so sorry. It seems Mrs. Oliver is out of the office. I guess she forgot to mention it to me. Did you have an appointment?" Before he could answer, she glanced at her watch and said, "To make amends, I can take you to lunch at our expense." Placing her hand on his upper arm, she added, "If it's all right with you, that is. She should be back by the time we return."

Blackridge looked at April for a moment, shrugged, and held out his arm. Smiling, April said, "Just let me get my purse, and we'll be off." She flipped the switch on the phone so it would ring in the back offices as she looped her arm through his and walked toward the elevator.

Luckily, April and Blackridge returned from lunch about ten minutes ahead of Nora. When she alighted from the elevator, she spotted Blackridge immediately. "John! How are you?" she asked, giving him a quick hug before tugging on his arm to lead him toward her office. "It's been ages since we've talked."

Turning back toward April, she said, "April, would you please fix John and me a cup of Robusta coffee from the special container I keep in the breakroom?" When he started to protest, she chastised him gently. "You know I have to drug you with caffeine before you loosen up with all the juicy gossip!" Laughing, she walked with him toward her office.

April tapped her foot impatiently as she waited for the coffee to brew. Hearing the elevator bell ding, she glanced at the pot before heading out to see who it was. By the time she returned, it was finished. Pulling two cups out of the cabinet, she filled them with coffee and placed them on a silver tray along with sugar. Reaching into the refrigerator, she grabbed a small pitcher of half-and-half and placed it on the tray.

As she headed for Nora's office, she walked carefully to keep the coffee from sloshing. She would never survive as a waitress. As she turned the corner into the office, she looked up and smiled at Nora. She didn't want to give John special attention in front of Nora. Besides, it would be better if John didn't perceive her as just another fan.

"Thank you, April," said Nora. Realizing Nora was not going to introduce her to John, she turned to leave. John didn't say a word.

When John was leaving, April made it a point to be away from her desk before he reached reception on his way out. Later she was walking down the hall to the restroom past all the offices.

"Can you believe it?" Donna Jarvis asked, a question April knew could definitely lead to valuable information or at least gossip. At the very least, it might be something she could store away for the future. She slowed to a halt, squatted in the hall and pretended to be fussing with her boots, all the while listening intently. She had no idea the conversation she was about to hear heralded a turning point in her life.

"Believe what?" asked Ginger. Despite having been with the company as long as Donna, Ginger Goodroe was still assisting Donna as an Associate Editor, although Nora did allow her to handle a few projects on her own. A shy and rather naïve woman, despite being in her thirties, it was not surprising her particular area of interest was young adult fiction. Donna Jarvis's was dark fantasy, making them a strange duo.

"That the great John Blackridge has dried up!" she replied, a definite note of triumph in her voice.

"That's terrible!" replied Ginger. Obviously Ginger was still in awe of John.

"Terrible, my ass! That stuff-shirt needs to be brought down a notch or two."

"But Nora seems to really like him. I heard them laughing in her office, and I heard her tell April to fix him coffee from her special blend that she doesn't let anyone else touch." Ginger sounded like she was on the verge of a breakdown, not knowing whether to be loyal to her mentor, Nora, or side with her boss.

Donna made a chuffing sound before upbraiding Ginger. "Sometimes, Ginger, I wonder how you made it this far. It's a wonder some con hasn't ripped you off for everything you own!" Before Ginger could reply, Donna continued, "Haven't you ever noticed he *never* stoops to talk to any of us, that he treats us like we're all clerical help? If it wasn't for us, his crappy writing wouldn't have made it beyond the slush pile. We *made* him! Don't you get it? He's nothing — just a name!"

April heard a book hit the desktop. She stood. She had heard what she needed to hear. Just as she passed the doorway, she heard Ginger remark, "Well, Nora doesn't seem to think so!" April chuckled as she heard Donna snort loudly in disgust.

****

Two weeks later, April picked up the phone at her desk, balancing it on her shoulder as she stirred her coffee. "Oliver & Company. How may I direct your call?"

"How about directing it to that lovely lady with whom I had the pleasure to dine a few weeks ago?"

Recognizing his voice right away, but choosing to play with him a little, April replied, "Since there are only women in this office, your request makes it difficult for me to help you."

Blackridge laughed loudly. "You are a force to be reckoned with, aren't you? Never make it easy on a guy. Is that your motto?"

Laughing softly, April replied, "Well, now that you mention it, you might be right on all counts."

"Just what I suspected. Listen. How would you feel about going to dinner with me? I have to attend a gala at a fellow author's house. His last book just broke all the records of his previous books so he's throwing a party. Would you like to be my date?"

April could barely contain her excitement. Things were moving along faster than she had expected. She had hoped to touch base with John within the next few weeks, if she hadn't heard from him, and present a proposal. This, however, was even better. There were bound to be lots of authors at this shindig and being John's date, she would surely meet most of them. The cherry on the top of this delicious event was that it should motivate John to find a story to help him out of his dry spell. An author never wanted to be yesterday's news.

Her dream was taking shape. Inhaling deeply, she could almost fill the power starting to fill her up again. "Why, Mr. Blackridge, I'd be glad to join you. What shall I wear?" asked April, letting her Southern drawl slip in.

Not a second of her performance had slipped by John. It was one of the things he liked about her — her capriciousness. Their lunch had convinced him he wanted to see more of her, but he knew she wasn't a woman to be taken lightly. She had her own mind and wasn't about to play second-fiddle to a man or anyone else for that matter. He knew he had to play it slowly, let her feel like she was pulling the strings. This could prove to be the best time he'd had in years. After telling April it was formal dress and getting her address, John arranged to pick her up at her apartment on Saturday night around seven o'clock.

April rushed home from work, barely taking time to kick off her shoes when she arrived. She headed straight for her library of storylines. She wondered what would be the best way to describe John's work. Was his genre thrillers or romance? There was always a lot of both in his books, and she knew he had a large fan base of romance readers who loved his books. Still, it was the thriller part of his books that was usually advertised, so it would probably be best to stick with that. She began her search to locate a storyline she could use to lure him into her web.

Should she approach him Saturday night after the party or wait until Sunday morning at breakfast? No, it was too early to let their relationship go that far. Besides, being too easily intimate with a prime player hadn't worked out so well in the past. No, she would invite him over for brunch on Sunday. Perfect. They would be on her turf, and she knew she could convince him she was the answer to his problems.

Chapter 9

"Did you enjoy the party?" John asked as he settled into the driver's seat of his Mercedes automobile. Fastening her seat belt, April cast a furtive glance toward John. Damn, he was handsome! He had escorted her around like she was the queen of England, introducing her to everyone. He never once indicated she was just the receptionist at Oliver & Company. He never even mentioned her credentials. The one time he was asked, he simply replied, "Oh, why spoil the surprise? It won't be long before you know exactly who she is!"

Everyone had laughed and accepted what he said at face value. She had managed to laugh along with them. What she had really wanted to do was drag him into the corner to ask what that remark was all about. Instead, she'd reined in her emotions and decided it was actually a useful introduction. It would make it look like John Blackridge knew about her plans all along — and approved of them! If it wouldn't have looked silly, she would have hugged herself right then and there.

At this moment, she felt like hugging John. Putting him off tonight would be harder than she thought because she couldn't think of anything she'd rather do than run her hands slowly down his back until she could feel the tight roundness of his butt. As she was imagining her next move, John cleared his throat.

"Fantasizing?" he asked, an enticing grin on his face.

Seriously taken aback by his ability to eavesdrop on her daydreams, she answered, "What? No! Why would you say that?"

"Well, you looked like you were definitely enjoying something," he replied.

"Oh, that! I was just reliving the evening. It was great meeting all those authors. People talk about them like they know them, but you never really see them like real people. You know what I mean?"

"Yes, I definitely know what you mean. Unfortunately, if you are one of those people, it can be distressing trying to live up to an image or even your past successes." A fleeting frown appeared, but he quickly changed the subject. "Well, we can grab a nightcap, or we can take you home. Which would you like?"

It was the perfect opportunity for her to invite him over for brunch the next day. It would let him know she wasn't planning to spend the rest of the evening or the night with him, but her fantasies wouldn't let her utter the words. He saved her the trouble of making a choice. "You look pretty tired. I think I ought to take you home."

"That sounds good," she replied. She slid down in the seat so her head was supported by the headrest and closed her eyes. She allowed her earlier fantasies to take flight. It had been a long time since she had been with someone. Since that "someone" had fired her, she had been a little too busy to test the waters. There was something about John, though. She hadn't been this turned on by anyone before, and she hadn't even kissed the man! Her body was already responding to the thought of his touch on her body. What would it be like when she could feel the warmth from his body against hers? Something unusual happened when he looked at her with those gray eyes of his, something she'd never experienced before. She could almost feel him caressing her, possessing her.

"Here we are," John announced as he pulled his car under the portico of her building. The doorman stepped out to open her door.

Stirring from her dreams, she said, "What? Oh, sorry. I guess I fell asleep." When she realized he wasn't getting out, she asked, "Do you want to come up?"

"No, I think you need some rest." He reached across the seat and kissed her on the cheek.

Stunned that her fantasies had just crashed and burned, April took a deep breath to clear her head of all the mental images she had conjured. "What about coming by for brunch tomorrow? Say around ten o'clock. I have something to talk with you about, which you might find very interesting."

John didn't answer for a moment. He was trying to figure her out. Acting like a desperate female was definitely not her style so it must be something else. "You do, eh? Should I ask or just wait and see?"

Feeling like her feet were back on solid ground, April smiled coyly. "Just wait and see," she replied as she shut the car door. Bending down, she waved before turning to enter the building.

****

The loud buzzing echoed through the bedroom. April raced to shut off the alarm clock in the kitchen. Wiping her hands on her apron, she slapped the button on the top of the portable clock before heading back toward the array of foodstuffs she was setting out for her brunch with John Blackridge.

Looking across the breakfast bar, April could see the morning sky with its promise of a new day. She hoped it didn't let her down. She wanted to be back in the game. She *needed* to be back in the game. She had been working toward her goal for the last nine months so it hadn't been too bad, but still, seeking after power could never be as satisfying as having it. She felt like everything was riding on today's brunch. What if he rejected her proposal? Worse, what if he told Nora about it? Oh, my God! She hadn't thought about that! She dropped onto the nearest bar stool. *Surely not—*

Shaking herself loose from such bleak thoughts, she vowed to use her considerable skills to manipulate John Blackridge into doing exactly what she wanted. After all, he was just a writer, not a high-powered businessman. She didn't know his background — which she probably needed to find out — but it was unlikely he had much experience using duplicity to get what he wanted. He seemed rather straightforward to her.

Looking around, she ticked off the items on her brunch menu. She had prepared for mimosas to drink, a concoction of champagne, orange juice, and Grand Marnier. She opened the refrigerator to make sure all three were chilling. Pulling a round silver tray out of the cabinet, she carefully placed on it the six huge, blueberry muffins she had bought from the bakery two streets over. The cream cheese and heavy cream ingredients resulted in a flavor which was unforgettable. She was tempted to eat one of them and call it breakfast, but she resisted.

What else? It would take about an hour to prepare and cook the quiche. She had prepared the crust for the veggie pizza last night, and it would take about 30 minutes to finish it up. She finished the fruit salad last night, also. Glancing at her watch, she saw she had three hours until John arrived. She could spend the next hour taking a bath and getting ready. It would leave her an hour and a half to finish up the quiche and the pizza with thirty minutes left over to set up the buffet.

Her bath should have relaxed her, but April could still feel tension lingering in her shoulders. Today would make the difference between her future being a paved road or a gravel one with potholes. Glancing at the clock, she prepared two mimosas and set them on the buffet just as the doorbell rang. She had instructed the doorman to let John into the building when he arrived. To make sure she was in control of the atmosphere, her plan was to greet John with a drink in hand. Fortunately, it was September and wasn't chilly enough for him to be wearing a jacket. So taking a deep breath, she shifted into her most radiant smile and walked toward the door with one of the mimosas. Opening the door, she lifted the mimosa toward him.

"Welcome! You're right on time," she remarked as she walked over to the buffet, picked up her own drink, and held it high for a toast. "Here's to bright futures!" she declared.

"Not a problem I've ever had, but I'll certainly toast to it anyway," replied Blackridge as he brought the glass to his lips. Licking his lips, he said, "Hey, this is great! You ought to be a bartender."

"How do you know I haven't been?" she teased, walking away from him and knowing he was watching her every move.

John cleared his throat. He knew she was once again putting on a great performance, but nevertheless, he found himself mesmerized by her skill — so fluid, so natural. The urge to applaud was compelling, but he couldn't risk applauding in case she thought he was mocking her. It might cut short this interesting diversion his life had taken. The irony was he knew April wanted him to be in the audience, caught up in the drama, being led by her every word and gesture. Instead, he was watching critically from stage left.

"Hungry?" she asked, picking up a plate and holding it out to him. Seeing him hesitate, she said, "Would you rather I fix it for you?" Before he could answer, she used the silver tongs to pick up a medium-sized piece of quiche and placed it on his plate. She used her fingers to maneuver a piece of the veggie pizza from the tray to his plate. "Fruit salad?" she asked. John nodded, and she placed a large scoop of the salad onto his plate before handing it to him.

****

"What do you mean you have a story proposal? You're not a writer. Do you really think you can just come up with storylines that are worth a damn without experience in the field?" Blackridge was incensed at her gall. His fascination of her manipulative skills vanished without a trace as his ego stormed out to defend its place.

April reached out to touch his arm, but he pushed out of her reach. Shocked, she asked, "What is wrong with you? I—"

"You ... you what? You think you can manipulate everyone who comes down the road? Oh, you're good, but you've gone too far this time!" He stood as if to make his point by towering over her.

The fire inside her started slowly as she looked at this handsome man, who was essentially the doorman to her new career, but who was going to be absent a few vital organs if he didn't back off. She rose from the sofa until she was standing so close to him she could feel his breath puffing onto the bridge of her nose.

"First of all, you big blowhard, if you'd put your ego in your back pocket long enough to listen to the rest of my proposal, you might just have to eat your words. I did not write these storylines. I did spend nearly a year reading and cataloguing storylines from the slush pile. You'd be surprised to discover that many of those who will never be writers do have enough imagination to come up with a good story. They just don't know how to put it into words anybody wants to read.

"Also, I may be manipulative, but I'm also damn smart! I can tell the difference between a story with promise and one without. After all, it's we ignorant readers who decide what to buy. We're the ones who decide if your great ideas suck or not!"

Chagrined, John stepped back a step. Maybe he should listen. He hadn't had a new book in quite a while. He might still be the darling of Oliver & Company at the moment, but this could change quickly if he failed to produce. The word was you're only as good as your last novel, but the truth was that even being on the bestseller list didn't mean anything if you couldn't produce the next novel before the spotlight faded.

"Okay, I'll listen," he said as he sat back down on the sofa, "but I'm not expecting much."

April ignored his lame attempt to regain the upper hand. Instead, she remained standing for a moment before walking across to the buffet to fix herself a mimosa. She didn't offer to make John one. Walking back across the room, she sat down in the chair opposite the sofa. She knew John wouldn't miss her point.

"Tell me, is it lack of a storyline that has you blocked?" she asked innocently.

"Who says I'm blocked?" he asked a bit too quickly.

"Duh! Everyone in the office," she replied. "Back to my question. Is it lack of a storyline?"

"Yes," he answered, feeling his ego slip further down into his back pocket.

"In that case, you're in luck because I have the solution. First, however, we need to discuss the conditions." April settled in more comfortably in her chair before presenting her deal to John.

"I intend to open my own press. I need authors, and you need a story to write if you want to stay on top of the book market."

Before she could continue, John muttered, "How do you intend to start your own press? Do you have a secret stash of money somewhere?"

"Maybe, but I may not need it. This is where you come in."

"Me? I'm not loaning you money to start a press."

"No, silly, you're going to *help* me start my own press!"

Moving to the front edge of the sofa cushion, John replied, "That will be a cold day in hell!"

"Well, I wouldn't be so quick to judge if I were you. How long have you been trying to write a new book?" Waving her hand to indicate she didn't expect an answer, April continued. "I can tell you that it's long enough the industry is starting to think of you as a has-been. No, don't argue. I hear the backroom rumors, so to speak. You are on your way out if you don't come up with a good novel in short order." April let him digest that juicy piece of information for a minute. John's face went slack as her bluntness dredged up the fear which had been stalking him for months.

"So what is your proposal?"

"After we sign a contract … just hang on," she said when she saw his mouth open." After we sign a contract, I will offer you three story outlines to choose from. Your contract will specify that you are now under contract to Center Stage Press and all books written by you from that time forward will be under contract to Center Stage. You will notify Nora Oliver you are no longer interested in being represented by her publishing house, and just so you know, your contract with me will also have a nondisclosure paragraph, preventing you from telling her where you are taking your business."

"I can't treat Nora that way," John said, looking at April like she was some sort of alien who had no idea of the way business relationships were handled.

"How are you going to feel about her when she dumps you because the industry is talking about how you can't come up with a new book?"

"I'll come up with something. Besides Nora wouldn't let a story like that see the light of day."

Laughing, April replied, "No, she wouldn't, but I would. Don't underestimate me, John. I've taken down men much bigger than you."

John stared at this woman sitting before him. She had everything going for her. She was attractive at her worst and beautiful at her best. Her hair was golden with natural highlights, and her eyes were brown with flecks of gold. With the sun coming through the window, she looked like an angel, but John was beginning to appreciate the meaning of *all that glitters is not gold.* Strangely, he was drawn to her strength even though he understood it came with a manipulative nature that could easily destroy him.

"I see your point," he said. April chuckled softly. "What are the other conditions because I know there are other conditions, and I'm sure they will emasculate me at the very least."

Laughing, April replied, "Don't be so maudlin. I don't want to emasculate you. I want you to be a part of this glorious adventure with me!"

"Do I get to walk upright?" he asked. "No leashes?"

"Only invisible ones, and you just might come to enjoy it," she purred.

Clearing his throat, John repeated, "So what are the other conditions?"

"Center Stage will have the standard royalty agreement with you, but I personally will receive 50% of your 15% royalty on this first book for the duration of my life. This will leave you with 7.5% and me with 7.5%." Since Blackridge had banked $2 million on his last book, it could be a sweet deal for her.

"I'm still not sure how you're going to pull this off," said John. "How can you produce my book with no money?"

"Don't worry. It will take you time to write your book. In the meantime, you're going to help me recruit at least two other major authors—"

"I'm what?" he exclaimed. "Why would I do that?"

Like a patient tutor, April explained, "Well, John, you have two choices: 1) stay with Nora and suffer the consequences when the industry realizes you've burned out; or 2) come in with me and ride this comet around the sun and back."

She had to be mental, he thought. No way a sane person would propose such a risky scheme. What if Nora found out? She wouldn't be able to even get a handout in this town. Yet, he had to admit he was intrigued by her panache, and he could think of worse things than being in cahoots with a woman who not only had looks that could silence a crowd, but also balls the size of Texas!

"What makes you think I can recruit other writers?"

"Get real! You know you're still the crème de la crème for right now. Authors are just people. They want to rub shoulders with you, hoping some of your success will rub off on them. You will make an excellent Pied Piper."

Shaking his head, John knew he was jumping off a cliff with a small parachute and no idea where the bottom was or if he would take flight before he was splattered across the ground below, but his adrenalin was at full force, and there was no turning back. "Okay, I'm in," he said.

Chapter 10

Center Stage Press

John Blackridge could not believe what had happened over the last week. April was true to her word. Once he signed that incredibly long contract — he wasn't sure if he hadn't signed away his first-born in this life and the next — she presented him with a storyline. She had promised him three, but she had concluded he only needed to have one at a time.

As he read over the first one, he was hooked. He was fired up to start writing before he even finished reading the outline. Concerned about the method used to develop the storyline, he questioned her about how close it was to a slush pile manuscript. April assured him she had simply used the ideas from storylines as triggers for developing similar storylines. She had changed the settings, the characters, the backgrounds, the triggering events, and the endings.

"Why did you even need the slush pile contributors if you're able to fabricate stories that are so completely different?"

"I'm a bloomer," she stated. Of course, John had no idea what that was. She quickly explained, "I have a fertile imagination, but it's not an initiating imagination."

"What does that mean?" His curiosity was aroused.

"It means I don't easily come up with ideas out of the blue, but give me a spark, and my imagination can take it places yours never would. I make it bloom!" she replied with a broad grin.

"So you're saying you didn't really use the exact storylines from the manuscripts; you just sort of used them as a starting point?"

"Yeah. Some I didn't even bother to get past the initial story setting because my imagination had already been ignited. Just out of curiosity, however, I did go back on several after I had written out my outline for the story to see where they had taken it. They never went in the same direction I did so I wouldn't worry about it."

John realized that April was much more talented than he had thought. Oh, he had known she was a master manipulator, but it seemed she was much more than a receptionist. It would serve him well to find out more about her.

****

Sitting in his house looking out across Lake Michigan, John considered what a lucky happenstance it had been for him to go to lunch with April that day. He wasn't really a ladies' man, so he didn't flirt with every woman he encountered. Truth be told, he wasn't really flirting with her that day; she had just intrigued him. During their lunch, it was so obvious she was a performance artist — the little touches, the well-timed laughter, and the thoughtful attentions of a confidante. If he'd been a little younger, he might have been taken in by her. Since he first hit the bestseller list, however, he had learned the manipulative ways of both women and men. If you had something they wanted, people would go to great lengths to get it, even if it meant embarrassing themselves in the process.

In this case, it just might turn out to be a win/win for them both. The storyline April had given him was rich with possibilities, and he could hardly wait to get started. He had been making notes constantly. Waiting in line at Starbucks, he was hit with a vision of his main character, right down to the scar on the back of his hand. Next thing he knew, he had grabbed a napkin and was scratching down notes. It had possessed him. He was excited in a way that hadn't happened since his very first novel. He felt young again, energized by his own passions.

Six months. This was his goal. He would commit to finishing the draft for his editor by the end of six months. Picking up the phone, he dialed April's number.

"Hello," she said with a note of hesitation in her voice. She knew it was John from the caller ID, but she wasn't expecting his call. Although confident in her plans, she knew a lot depended on how invested John was in them.

"April, it's John."

"I figured that out," she remarked with a chuckle.

Laughing, he replied, "Right, caller ID. Anyway, I just wanted to update you."

"Update me?" She couldn't imagine what he was talking about.

"Yeah. I want you to know that the storyline you gave me has set my imagination on fire!" April laughed in relief. "I'm serious. I can't think of anything else. I'm making notes on it standing in line at the coffee shop, waiting for the subway, any place I'm standing still for more than two seconds—"

"That's great, John, and you're welcome," she interrupted his excited babble, thinking he was just calling to thank her for the storyline.

"No, I called to tell you that I'm setting a six-month deadline to finish the book and have it ready for the editor."

April could hear the excitement in his voice. "Are you sure? We need this to be the best book you've ever written if we're going to get off the ground running with this press."

"I'm sure, April. I haven't been this excited about a novel in a long time." April was silent for a moment, contemplating what this accelerated time line meant. "April?"

"I was just thinking that this means we need to sit down and talk about a couple of things. First, you need to move forward on severing your connections with Oliver & Company." John flinched, not because he had regrets but because he hated conflict.

"Also, there's the issue of the two additional authors you need to help bring on board. Moving the time line up this much, we need to identify our targets and start working on them. They'll need time to get their books ready, too. I want to bring the books out in succession, giving each book time to shine before hitting the market with another."

"Hey, I've been thinking about that. I think I know the ones I want to contact," John replied enthusiastically.

Thinking quickly, April said, "Let's meet and talk about them. You can fill me in on their histories and why you think they're the best candidates. Then we can lay out the best plan for approaching them."

"Sounds great! When and where?"

John's behavior was throwing April a little off-center. She hadn't expected him to get on board so fast. "You certainly are gung-ho!" she laughed.

"I'm a writer, April. When I get the opportunity to write a great story, I'm on board, even if it's with the devil himself."

"Hey!" she retorted.

"Nothing personal, April, but as long as I can do what I love doing, that's all that matters to me. I don't like being used — no don't pretend you're not using me," he said, drowning out her protest, "but as long as you're not the only one benefitting, I can live with it."

"Well," April said, "in that case, we're in business. I want to win, and the only way to do that is if you win, too!"

"So, where and when?" John asked again.

"How about my place tomorrow evening?"

"Works for me. See you around seven o'clock," he replied before hanging up.

April sat down on her sofa where her attention was drawn to the calm waters of Lake Michigan. Knowing John's apartment fronted on the lake, she wondered if he was also watching the waves lap gently onto the shore. She had never expected him to succumb to her plans so easily. At brunch he had been resistant at first; of course, he had eventually yielded to her veiled threats just as she had expected. What she had not expected was this full-on commitment so quickly. Should she be suspicious? Was it possible he and Nora were in cahoots? Shaking her head, April dismissed the idea immediately. John had signed a legal contract with her, and besides, he wouldn't want the industry to know he was blocked, that he hadn't been able to come up with a storyline on his own. No, she thought, he was on board because she was damn good at manipulating people to get what she wanted.

Chapter 11

God, it had been a long day! April was finding it more and more difficult to stay focused on her work at Oliver & Company. Her mind was whirling with all the things she needed to do. If she and John were going to launch Center Stage Press in just over six months, there were hundreds of details to handle. She really needed to quit and devote herself full time, but it would cut her off from the industry, and she wasn't ready to take that step. There were still contacts she needed to make

Another reason for staying was because she wanted to see the effect her actions were having on Nora's company. Nora seemed almost prescient about what the future held. Her moods were totally unpredictable these days, upsetting everyone in the office. Donna had already threatened to resign, but Ginger had talked her down. April had made a note, wondering if Donna might be a good candidate for an editorial position later, but she'd have to give this some thought. She didn't want a prima donna on staff.

April jumped when a door slammed close by. Peeking around the corner, the only closed door was Nora's. April knew John had not contacted Nora yet, but something was going on because Nora's emotions were all over the charts. Frowning, April wondered if there was any way Nora could have found out what was happening but dismissed the idea as impossible. Satisfied, she picked up her purse, shut off the front desk phone, and headed for the elevator and home.

John was coming over tonight, and she wanted to stop at The Lakeside Bistro and pick up some carryout. They had great Southern barbecue, and she was in the mood for comfort food.

April was struggling to get in the front door of her condo when she heard the elevator ding. She paid it no attention because the bags of barbecue were slipping through her fingers. Choosing the barbecue over her keys, she let the keys drop to the floor to get a better grip on the bags. Before she had time to reorganize everything, someone reached past her and plucked the keys off the floor. Jumping back, she nearly dropped her precious cargo.

"Who—John! What are you doing here? It's just barely six o'clock, isn't it? she asked, trying to get a bead on her watch.

"I couldn't reach you on your phone, so I thought I'd drop by to see if you wanted to go out for dinner first, but I see you've already taken care of it," he said. Before she could answer, he asked, "Is there enough for two?"

April nodded, "Well, it just so happens I do have enough for two!" As she returned his grin, she wondered why she felt like a school girl cornered at her locker by the most popular guy in school. Trying to shift the mood, she glanced at her keys, dangling from his hand. "Are you going to use those, or are we going to eat in the hall?"

Laughing at her spirit, he unlocked the door and held it while she eased through. April hurried through to the kitchen bar and gently placed the bags on the counter. Watching her shoulders relax, he asked, "What do you have in there — gold?"

"In a manner of speaking," she replied as she pulled plates down from the cabinet and set them on the bar. Dragging the bags toward her, she pulled out tin after tin until John had to ask, "Are we expecting anyone else?"

"Of course not! If we were, there would be at least five more tins," she declared. John could hardly wait to see what was in all of them. The aroma was wonderful. His growling stomach agreed.

"I see you're ready for some comfort food. Your stomach sounds like a whiny child."

"Excuse me?" he bantered. "How can you say such a thing to a man as sophisticated as I am? I'll have you know I've eaten in the finest restaurants in this town as well as in New York, and no one has ever accused me or my stomach of being like a whiny child." John had walked around the bar as he talked and was now standing next to April.

Looking up at him, she felt an energy radiating from him that as a sensual woman, she liked, and as a businesswoman, she could use to her advantage. Strangely, however, she found herself thinking differently about him. She couldn't quite define it because it was an unfamiliar sensation. She kept reminding herself he was just a means to an end, no different than Brandon or Jeffrey. At least that was what her head told her.

John reached out and touched her arm as she was trying to remove the top from one of the tins. "Let me do that," he said. "It will be exciting to discover what lies beneath each of these."

April felt herself shudder slightly after he removed his hand. Forcing a smile, she handed him the tin. "Help yourself," she said. "Since you've become the chef, I think I'll freshen up." He nodded absently, and she headed for the bedroom where she plopped down on the bed.

This can't be happening, she thought. *I'm acting like some school girl. There's too much at stake for me to lose control now.* After sitting a few minutes longer and rehearsing her goals in her mind, April went to the bathroom and spritzed her face. Shaking her head firmly to clear out any stray thoughts that shouldn't be there, she returned to the living room.

Dinner resting heavily in their stomachs, April and John were sitting on the sofa, each drinking a glass of wine. April absently swirled the wine around in her glass as she gazed out at the lights dotted along the shore line of Lake Michigan. She caught herself thinking about the romantic elements surrounding her: wine, the lights along the lake twinkling like candle flames against the night, and John.

"A bestseller for your thoughts," John said quietly.

April turned her gaze on him for a second before laughing at his remark. "Speaking of bestsellers, tell me about the two candidates for our team." John liked the way she described them as a team. Of course, he knew April was in charge, and he suspected his longevity with Center Stage Press depended completely on the success of his new novel. Knowing the way he felt about this latest novel, however, he couldn't imagine its being anything other than a success. Regardless, no reason not to enjoy himself.

"Well, the first person who came to my mind was Devon McNally," John said. April frowned. She knew he was a new writer with only one book under his belt, not necessarily the kind of candidate she was expecting. "I can tell by the look on your face that you don't like my suggestion, but wait until you hear my reasoning," John added.

"You're right. He's not what I expected."

"Here's the thing. Yes, he is a first time novelist, but his book has been a bestseller. I've read it, and I have to tell you he definitely has writing chops. There's nothing contrived about his talent. He has plenty more books where that one came from."

"What makes you think he would be interested in leaving Nora's stable?" April knew that initiates were often devotees of their publisher, and she did not want some overzealous newcomer showing her hand to Nora before she was ready.

"Trust me on this one. I spoke with him the other day—"

"What! You spoke to him about this before talking to me?" April pushed herself to the edge of the sofa cushion.

"Calm down, will you?" John insisted. "I didn't talk to him about this. I was just chitchatting with him at a friend's house. You know, general stuff. Of course, with authors, general stuff means anything related to your books or your publisher. Everything else is out there on the fringes somewhere."

"Okay. So what did he say that makes you think he's a good candidate?"

"He was grousing about the low royalty Nora is giving him. Of course, it's a standard new writer royalty, but since his book has become such a huge hit, he thinks she should increase the royalty — if not on this book, on the next."

"Has he approached her?" April was beginning to follow John's reasoning.

"Yes, and she told him that having one bestseller was not considered proof of his potential as a long term asset. Needless to say, he has his knickers in a wad." John reached out for the wine bottle to refill his glass. "Would you like a refill?" he asked.

"Sure," she replied. "Do you think he's at the point where he would leave her? I mean, for a new writer, their publisher is like a pacifier — they represent the assurance that all is well in their world."

"Oh, rest assured I am familiar with that feeling. However, I think Devon has worked himself up enough that if you — pardon the cliché — give him an offer that he can't refuse, he would be here in a nanosecond."

April stared into her wine glass as she considered what she would offer Devon McNally. "I'm willing to offer him 15% royalty on his next two novels with the proviso that they must each sell in eighteen months as many copies as his debut novel did in its first year. If not, all his royalties will drop to 9% until he can prove his value to Center Stage Press as a long term asset. How do you think he would respond to this?" April had watched John's eyes closely as she recited the offer. He had not flinched at the final condition as she thought he might.

Now he was smiling. "I think you'll have a new team member."

"You don't think he'll balk at the 9%?" April preferred to bring all potential issues out into the open.

"Hell, no! First of all, it's more than he's getting now. Second, every writer believes their next novel is a bestseller. That illusion alone will make him discount even the possibility of its becoming an issue. Besides, I agree with the illusion. I think his next two novels will be bestsellers."

April smiled. "One down and one to go — at least for now." She rose and headed for the kitchen.

"Are you still hungry?" asked John, unable to imagine anyone being hungry after the barbecue feast they had enjoyed. Pulled pork, baked beans, coleslaw, fried okra, corn on the cob, not to mention the onion garnish, which he could still taste, despite the red wine.

"Just going to get an orange Creamsicle. It helps cleanse my palate after all those spicy, rich foods."

"That's a new one on me. Sort of a down home version of sorbet?" he asked, one corner of his mouth tilting upward.

April laughed. "I'm a Southerner, remember? We may not always take the fancy route, but we never sacrifice function for form. If it works, it works — doesn't matter if it conforms to the norm or not. Want one?"

"Absolutely, that onion refuses to move on."

Grabbing a second Creamsicle, April headed for the sofa. "So, tell me about your second candidate."

Unwrapping the tasty treat as he talked, John continued, "I think you'll like this one. Her name is Laney Whitcombe—"

"*The* Laney Whitcombe?" April was shocked. She was not only a bestselling author, she was a top contender in the entire marketplace, rivaling names like Dean Koontz and Janet Evanovich in numbers.

John grinned, knowing he would score big with April if he could bring Laney into the fold. "Yes, *the* Laney Whitcombe."

"Why in the world would she even consider breaking away from her publisher?" April's heart was in her throat. This could be the pièce de résistance. With both her and John on board, Center Stage Press would be out of the gate and surpassing the other small presses before they even realized they had competition.

"Well, you know she's been quite successful writing romance novels. The problem is she wants to write more mainline mystery novels without romance being a primary component." John paused to take a bite of his Creamsicle. "Hey, I think this thing really works. I can't taste the onion anymore."

"To hell with the Creamsicle! Tell me about Whitcombe. Am I wrong or isn't she with one of the Big Six publishers?

John couldn't help smiling at her impatience. He was tempted to draw it out as long as he could, but he wasn't certain how far he could go with her yet. "Yes, she is. She's talked with them about her desire to change her genre, but they're refusing to consider publishing any books other than her romance series."

"Does she have a binding contract with them for all her books or for a certain period of time?" April was afraid to get too excited, but she couldn't stop the tingle working its way up her back.

"That's what's so great about it. Laney was very meticulous in looking after her interests when she signed on with them. Unlike most new writers, she made sure she had a good lawyer and struck a deal that's been gold for her, and in the long run, gives her the upper hand.

"She struck a deal for ten books in the series, but after that, her contract would be on a one book at a time basis. I guess the publisher figured she wouldn't last past ten books and didn't expect her to be the whirlwind success she became. Anyway, now she's in the position of calling the shots. They want her all right, but they want her to abide by the terms of their bottom line, which is the certainty that her romance books sell. They're not willing, it seems, to take a chance on a new genre even on a one book commitment."

"Wow! That's dumb."

"You know that, and I know that, but the big guys sometimes lose sight of the power behind their products — the authors — because they're so homed in on the bottom line. In this case, it could be good for us," John noted. April liked his use of the word *us* though she tried to ignore the sensations fluttering through her.

"Do you really think she's open to a change?" April asked hesitantly.

"I definitely do. She's a friend of mine. I talked to her last night to feel her out. Don't worry. I didn't mention Center Stage Press. Anyway, she's quite agitated about it all."

April could hardly contain her excitement. Everything was coming together. She had known it would, just not so quickly. "She can write whatever she wants at Center Stage Press. I'm a firm believer people will read whatever is good. True, not all her romance fans will follow her, but there are a lot of mystery readers out there looking for a new source of entertainment." April inserted the Creamsicle stick into her mouth and sucked up the last remaining sherbet that was stuck to the stick. Watching her titillating behavior, John chose to attack the remains of his Creamsicle from the side.

"Okay, I'm onboard with both of the candidates, but before we approach them, you need to deal with Nora." John winced as he rose to take his stick to the kitchen. April noticed. "Is there a problem?" she asked, eyebrows raised.

Clearing his throat, John replied, "No problem. When do you want me to talk with her?"

"Tomorrow." Eyes narrowed, she asked, "You're not trying to

back out, are you?" April didn't think this was the case at all. After all, he had a contract, and he was all excited about bringing in the two candidates they'd just discussed. No, it was something else.

"Well, I'm not looking forward to it, but I know it has to be done. You have to understand, April, that she believed in me when no one else did. It's like that pacifier analogy you used earlier." John sighed.

"John, let me tell you something — something I'm amazed you haven't figured out as long as you've been in the business. Nora may be a small press, but she's no different than the big publishing houses. Her only loyalty is to her bottom line. I'm sure she was different in the beginning. A lot of small presses probably start out with stars in their eyes, thinking they're going to be involved with the great literature of the ages. Eventually, however, the business end of the dream takes over, and they have to start analyzing their ROI. So an author's talent is simply measured in terms of the potential return on their investment.

"This same mindset trickles down to agents as well. You're probably not aware since you haven't needed an agent in a while, but today you see comments in agent directories like 'if you don't already have a financially successful book, don't bother to submit.' They're already calculating what kind of return they want for their 10%.

"Oh, not everyone is like that, of course, but I *can* tell you Nora is apparently having some financial difficulties, and her bottom line is her priority at the moment. If you don't produce, you're no more important to her now than last year's phone book."

"You're right. I've just always hated conflict. I'm a big boy, however, and I will talk with her tomorrow." Pausing for a moment, John asked the question that had been skulking at the back of his mind. "What would you have done if I was tied into a long term contract with Nora. I mean, what if I owed her more books?"

April smiled. "I guess I would have had to take Nora down first. Then your contract wouldn't have been an issue, would it?" John had no doubt she would have done exactly that. "So, let's make arrangements to meet with our two candidates this week. Do you have any place other than my house where we could meet privately?"

"I belong to a country club. They have private meeting rooms, and it's not a gathering place for writers, which is why I joined. I can't talk books all the time."

"Fine," she replied. "You set it up for Saturday if you can. Let's leave at least two hours between meets. Okay?"

John nodded. He was grappling with his feelings about this woman. She had once told him she had taken down bigger men than he was. He believed her. Yet, there was something there under all the bravado, something sweet and sensual. He could feel it reaching out to him at times. It had been a long time since he had met a woman with such spirit. His feelings about Nora were of no consequence really; this was his path now. He had never felt this strongly about anything else except his decision to be a writer.

Chapter 12

April could hear their voices from down the hall. Nora was practically screaming at John Blackridge. Heading down the hall toward the break room, April hoped to hear both sides of the conversation, but as Nora's volume continued to increase, she wasn't sure there were two sides at this point.

As she got closer to Nora's office, she spotted the entire gang of editors hovering in the door to their bullpen area where they normally gathered to discuss manuscript submissions. Donna Jarvis was up front, of course, along with her sidekick, Ginger Goodroe. Perched close behind them were Lindsey Brown, Sandra Lacy, and Jean Wilson. Jean fascinated April. She rarely looked any different than she had the day April arrived on the job. Today she even seemed to be wearing the same outfit. Time had shown her to be as mean as a junkyard dog, too, so April had deliberately steered clear of her. Strangely enough, Donna didn't even seem to notice Jean. Probably no room for two alpha females in Donna's vision of her world, thought April.

"What's going on, ladies?" April asked. "I could hear the screeching out in reception."

Donna motioned furiously for her to come over to them. April complied. "Sh-h! It seems Mr. High-and-Mighty is walking away from Oliver & Company. Well, we didn't actually hear him say that, but judging from the invectives Nora is spouting and the few intelligible phrases in-between, that's what we've gathered."

"Isn't he one of the prime authors here?" asked April innocently.

Donna snorted. "He thinks he is anyway. Frankly, I'll be glad to see him go."

At that moment, they all heard Nora shout, "Get out, you ungrateful SOB!"

"Quick, scatter!" whispered Donna rather forcefully. The editors all scrambled back into their bullpen. April moved casually up the hall toward reception. She was about ten feet past the doorway when John was unceremoniously tossed out of Nora's office. He came to a halt in the middle of the hall facing the door. He jumped involuntarily when Nora slammed it with the force of an explosion.

April hurried to reception so she would have a minute with him before he left. When John appeared, she smiled. "I won't ask how it went," she said, quietly.

"Well, it was a little more melodramatic than I expected— definitely a side of Nora I've never seen before," John whispered, shaking his head in disbelief.

"What did I tell you?" April inquired. "If she really cared as much about your future as she does her bottom line, she wouldn't have reacted that way." Hearing Nora's door open, April raised her voice to normal levels. "Is there anything I can get you before you leave, Mr. Blackridge?" she asked, flicking her eyes toward the hall.

John picked up on her cue. "No, April, I think Oliver & Company has done about all it can for me," he said, just as Nora appeared around the corner.

"Are you still here?" she asked.

"Just waiting on the elevator," he said.

"There are stairs, you know," she retorted before walking away.

John looked at April and rolled his eyes. April pulled her lips down over her teeth to keep from laughing — not from laughing at John, but from laughing with joy. It was official. John was now her client with no strings attached.

****

As April approached her building that evening, she noticed a man loitering outside the entrance. She wasn't particularly worried since the building had a doorman. Coming closer, she realized it was John. Surprised to see him standing there, she wondered if something had happened since earlier at the office. Before she could ask, he declared, "Well, I think you owe me a dinner."

"Me? Why?"

"The fact I survived that skirmish this afternoon for one."

"Okay. What's the other reason?" she asked.

"Huh? Oh, because I'm such good company, and besides, I need to let you know about the schedule for Saturday."

"You can't do that now?" She couldn't help giving him a hard time.

"No, I'm starving, and I don't think clearly on an empty stomach." Just because April was now his publisher, John was not intimidated.

"Didn't you eat lunch?"

"No, I sat in the coffee shop, saturating myself with caffeine and wondering if I've lost my mind," he stated.

Now he had her attention. Even though she had him by the family jewels, the last thing she needed right now was for him to start doubting his decision. She still needed to bring the other two candidates on board. Obviously, he had made the appointments, but she needed him to be in a persuasive state of mind or she could lose them.

"Have you?" she asked calmly.

"At first I thought I had, but then I realized it was just the aftermath of Nora's unexpected outburst. It was a few points up the Richter Scale from what I was expecting. Once I decompressed, I knew I had done the right thing." April sighed inwardly. "Are we going to eat or not?" John demanded.

Hooking her arm in his, she asked, "What did you have in mind?"

Walking around the corner from her building, John guided her into The Lakeside Bistro. "Are you a barbecue fan now?" she asked.

"Just thought this was a good night for comfort food," he replied. Seeing her shocked expression, he said, "You're not the only one who craves comfort food, you know."

Laughing, she replied, "That I know. I just never pictured you as being one of those people."

"There's a lot you don't know about me ... despite your careful investigations," he added, glancing sideways at her before informing the hostess there would only be two of them.

April watched his profile as they waited for their table. What was it about him that made it so easy to talk about anything? Most men she'd known had been absorbed in their own worlds, paying scant attention to hers. Of course, this had made it much easier to manipulate them, even Jeffrey. Unlike Brandon, Jeffrey had paid attention to her sexually, but he recognized her business sense. He never suspected she could be a danger to him. Of course, it turned out Elisa was the true danger, except to her. Never again would she ignore significant others; it didn't take more than once for her to learn her lesson.

Their wait was short, and they were soon seated at a nice table near the windows, slightly separated from the other tables by a planter. *Very cozy*, thought April. The waiter was at their table before they even had time to settle in. After ordering, April adjusted her napkin in her lap, waiting to see how John would begin their conversation. She sensed he felt the same energy between them and wondered if he would pursue it. Would he, instead, plunge right into the business reason for this dinner engagement?

As she wondered what his opening gambit would be, John studied her. He was torn by the reality of his professional life at the moment and by the feelings developing for this strong-willed, beautiful woman, who was like a rose — beautiful to view and fragrant to smell, but treacherous to touch unless you had a scheme for avoiding the pricks and eventual blood-letting. He would have to move carefully, but his heart was telling him it would be worth it.

When April looked up from her napkin, she saw this goofy grin on John's face. She tilted her head, raising her eyebrows inquisitively and holding out for his opening line.

"I was just thinking how crazy this moment is," observed John. "Here I am, after firing my publisher, sitting with my new publisher, who works for my old publisher, preparing to discuss the launching of a new small press — one, I might add, I suspect my new publisher envisions as the instrument of ruin for my old publisher."

April burst out laughing. "Well, when you put it that way, it does sound a bit crazy."

"Yes, it does," he replied. "I think I'm ready for a little crazy in my life though," he replied, gazing into her eyes as he spoke. April squirmed, despite her resolve not to react should their conversation take a personal path.

John abruptly changed the subject. "I have the appointments set up for Saturday. We'll meet Devon first at two o'clock and Laney at four o'clock. The place shouldn't be as crowded indoors in the afternoon. Does that work for you?" he asked just as the waiter arrived. April nodded.

After dinner, John walked April home and left her at the entrance with a quick, gentlemanly peck on the cheek. For the first time in a long time, April felt off-balance. John was like a bouncing ball. She never knew where he would land next. Did he really feel the connection between them or was she imagining things?

Chapter 13

Last night was a restless one for John. Today he and April would be talking with Devon and Laney. They were his friends, at least Laney was. Devon was still more of an acquaintance. He was truthful with April about them, but now that it was nearing show time, apprehension had kept him awake most of the night. He couldn't even concentrate on his new novel yesterday, which was another reason he was unnerved. His whole career seemed to be balancing on what happened today and in the next six months. He felt like he had walked out on a limb with only two options: hang on for dear life or crash and burn. He was too old to crash and burn. He didn't think the magic of the phoenix would work for him like it had in his youth.

****

April yawned, glanced at the clock, and leaped out of bed. She had slept like a baby. Today was the moment when all the ingredients for her future success would be placed in a decorative box, tied with a big, beautiful, poufy bow, and presented to her. What other small press started out with three powerhouses like John Blackridge, Laney Whitcombe, and Devon McNally as its first three clients? John and Laney were veterans, and although Devon was a rookie, he was a damn successful one. Besides, she trusted John's instincts about his future as a writer. Nothing she had ever done had felt like this. Excitement was bubbling up inside her like with a kid at Christmas.

The morning passed quickly, and April hurried downstairs to wait for John to pick her up. They had decided to go together since April didn't know where the country club was located. He picked her up a bit early so they headed for the country club bar first.

John had chosen the country club because it was not a writers' hangout, so April was shocked when John went to the restroom to overhear two guys' conversation.

"...Nora's going off the deep end, I think." Sitting at the end of the bar, she could easily hear them. Catching the name Nora, April thought it had to be someone else until she heard the reply.

"Yeah. I heard John Blackridge jumped ship the other day. He's been with her a long time. He must know something the rest of us don't for him to leave her just like that."

"I can't seem to get the skinny on what's going on, but there's something, trust me."

April was getting nervous, hoping John didn't return too quickly. *Who are these guys?*

"My boss would probably give me the front page of the business section and a byline if I could get the scoop on this."

They're reporters, thought April. *Oh, God!* She grabbed her purse and hurried out of the bar before John could return. She rushed to the area in front of the men's room to wait. Tapping her foot, she kept glancing down the hall to make sure the two men did not come out of the bar.

"Miss me?" John asked.

Frowning, she grabbed him by the arm. "Which way to the meeting room? Hurry!" she insisted.

"Hey, what's wrong?" he asked.

"Which way?" she insisted.

"All right, already! It's this way," he snapped. He pointed to his left.

Breathing a sigh of relief they did not have to pass by the bar, April pulled him down the hall. "Which one?"

"The Columbia Room." Before he could say another word, she barreled into the room and pushed the door closed behind them.

"What in the hell is wrong with you?" John asked, not sure whether to be worried or annoyed.

"Two guys, two reporters mind you, in the bar talking about Nora and you." April stopped to catch her breath. "They're looking for a scoop on what's happening to Nora's company. They think you know since you left there after all this time. If they had seen us together ..." April didn't continue. She left John to read between the lines. "Do Devon and Laney know which room we're meeting in?"

"Yeah. I emailed them directions."

"Thank God neither one of us will have to leave this room." April took a deep breath and exhaled slowly.

Looking at her quizzically, John asked, "Do you really think they would know who you are?"

"Not right now, but if they see us together and later they come by the office to interview Nora, who do you think they'll see first? Not to blow my own horn, but I'm not *that* forgettable!" John laughed. "It's not funny! We have to close the deal with Devon and Laney, or we're both screwed, and something like this could do it.

"What do you think would happen if Nora found out what we're up to? She would blackball both of us before we can even get started. Without Devon and Laney, we have no leverage — not that you don't have clout, John, but there's power in numbers, especially the numbers of sales the three of you represent."

There was a knock on the door. Still worried about the reporters, April motioned John to step to one side as she opened the door. A tall man, looking to be about twenty-five, stood there. He had auburn-colored hair with blue eyes and a rather appealing splash of freckles across his nose and cheeks. He wasn't attractive really, but all his features cooperated to make him appealing.

Looking confused, he said, "I beg your pardon. I must be in the wrong place. I was supposed to meet a friend of mine, John Blackridge," he muttered as he turned to leave.

Grabbing hold of his arm, she said, "You must be Devon McNally."

Startled that this stranger would know his name, Devon said, "You have me at a disadvantage, ma'am. Do you know Mr. Blackridge?"

By this time, John had walked to the door. "Come on in, Devon, and we'll get started."

"Get started?" he inquired. Looking at April, he added, "I thought you and I were just going to brainstorm about my situation with my publisher."

"Oh, we are, Devon."

"Then may I ask who you might be, ma'am?"

April was amused by his gentlemanly charm but answered him quickly. "I may be the answer to your problems." Devon looked at John, who smiled and nodded.

They pulled out a few chairs from the stack near the wall and unfolded one of the tables.

"Devon, when we talked the other day, you said you felt you deserved a better royalty than you're getting with Oliver & Company. Is this still correct?"

Before John could take a breath, Devon jumped right in. "Absolutely! The more I think about it, the madder I get. Oh, I know all the so-called reasons for the royalty I'm receiving, but I believe results should be taken into consideration. How many debut novels sell as many books as mine has?" Devon was on a roll. April nudged John with her foot when he started to interrupt him. Let him get his emotions worked up, she thought. Then he'll be ripe for the picking. After a few minutes of ranting about the injustice of it all, Devon wound down. April glanced at John and nodded.

"Devon, I have to ask you to sign a piece of paper before we get started."

Puzzled, Devon asked, "What kind of paper? I thought we were just brainstorming here."

"In a way, we are, but if you recall, the lady here told you she may be the answer to your problem. We're not ready to disclose our plans yet, and we need to make sure you don't either. So the bottom line is this: how badly do you want a better deal for your writing?" John paused to let it sink in. Devon stared at him for a moment before turning his gaze to April. She held her ground against his intense scrutiny, never flinching. She saw the flicker in his eyes when his decision was made.

"Okay, what do I need to sign?" John pushed the non-disclosure statement across the table. Devon scrawled his name at the bottom without even reading it.

He's mine, thought April.

John turned toward April. "Do you want to explain the situation to him?"

"Absolutely," she replied. "Devon, my name is April Saunders. I am the owner of Center Stage Press—"

"Never heard of it," he stated.

"No, but you will," she said, "you and the rest of the publishing industry. John here is our first author. Hopefully, you will be our second, and we have a third who will likely be coming aboard later today. She is a powerhouse as well."

Devon puffed up a little at being included as a powerhouse. His ego was already on board, which did not go unnoticed by the master manipulator seated across from him. "So, Devon, here is my offer to you. Your debut novel is currently part of Oliver & Company, and you have a 7% royalty. Is that correct?"

Devon snorted derisively before replying, "Yes, ma'am."

"Well, I can't change that. However, I can offer you 15% royalty on your next two books with the proviso they must each sell in eighteen months as many copies as your debut novel did in the first year. If not, all your royalties will drop to 9% until you can prove your value to Center Stage Press as a long term asset. How does that sound?"

Devon pulled his bottom lip to one side and clamped his upper teeth over it while he was thinking. "It sounds great, ma'am. I only have one question. What about my contract with Nora Oliver?"

April's heart leaped into her throat. *How could she have forgotten to ask John about Devon's contract? They had discussed Laney's in great detail—why not Devon's?* She flashed back to that day and realized she had been distracted by the mystique flowing from John, a charm which sometimes made it difficult for her to stay on point. In the future she would have to be more alert to when his influence was distracting her. She couldn't afford to let her guard down if she was going to succeed.

"John?" she asked, her ire seeping into her voice.

"Devon, I'm pretty sure you signed Nora's standard contract for a new author. She has not committed to you for more than this first book, correct?"

"That's right," Devon replied. April exhaled in relief. "But she has my new contract ready for me to sign. She's been trying to get me to come in for the last week, but I've been so angry about the percentages I didn't go in."

"Well, then, there's no problem. You simply don't sign it," said April.

"What do I tell her? I mean, if I can't disclose what we're doing, what do I say?"

John spoke up. "Just tell her you've decided to take your chances on finding another publisher who will better appreciate you."

"But what if she decides to give in to my earlier demands? I mean, she did take a chance on me the first time."

April looked at John. "What did I tell you about the pacifier?" Devon looked confused.

John explained. "April and I were discussing earlier that for a new novelist, his first publisher is like a pacifier. She represents security. She was his gateway into the industry. However, Devon, if you want to get ahead in this industry, you have to look out for yourself. You have to be willing to take chances if it looks like it will benefit you financially as a writer. Your publisher is not concerned about your financial future except as it affects hers."

"Does that profile include you?" Devon asked April.

"To some degree, yes," she replied. "The difference for you is that you would be getting in on the ground floor. My first three clients will be my golden circle. No one will surpass you for the long term unless you consistently bomb or quit taking the business seriously. Then I'll have to get rid of the unnecessary weight. As long as you perform and show your support for Center Stage Press, however, you have nothing to worry about."

Devon sat quietly for a few moments. April and John kept silent. "All right. I will sign with you. What do I do next?"

It was all April could do not to leap up and do a happy dance. Two down and one to go. Instead, she pulled the contract out of her slim briefcase and handed it to Devon. "Read it carefully," she said as she rose to get a glass of water. Someone had left a bucket of ice with a pitcher of water on the bar. John joined her.

"What do you think?" he whispered.

"I think we're on our way. You probably need to coach him about confronting Nora and remind him about the nondisclosure." They stood with their backs to the bar, watching Devon peruse the contract.

Finally, he scrawled his name on the last sheet and looked up. "What now?" he asked. April was pleased he was so compliant. The last thing she needed was someone who had to be constantly handled.

"Since John has already experienced walking away from Oliver & Company, he's going to give you some pointers. You will need to do this on Monday. One last thing: when you come into the office, you will see me. I am currently working the reception desk there. You will not acknowledge me in any way except as the receptionist. Do you understand?"

Devon's face was in flux. His mouth gaped open for a moment before he snapped it shut, a movement which seemed to push his eyebrows to the middle of his forehead. Next, his eyes started to blink rapidly.

"Are you okay?" April asked as Devon exhaled loudly. "Are you going to hyperventilate? Do we need to find a paper bag?" She knew he was fine. She just wanted him to realize how silly he was acting.

"No, I'm fine. I guess you just took me by surprise, ma'am. I never took you for a traitor."

"Excuse me!" she retorted, her angry surfacing. "I'll have you know, Devon, that I am no traitor. I came to this town with the intention of having my own press." This was a lie, but he didn't have to know it. "I have poured my heart and soul into preparing for this. I went to work at Oliver & Company for some on-the-job experience and to make some contacts. Of course, I didn't tell her of my dreams. That would have been rather stupid, don't you think? She didn't nurture me or help me move up in the industry. Did you not hear me when I said I was her *receptionist*?"

April took a breath, and Devon stepped in quickly. "I'm so sorry. I don't know why I said that. I can understand what you're saying. I'm sort of wet behind the ears when it comes to business. How else would you learn the ropes unless you worked in the industry. Right?" he asked. April could see he was genuinely regretful he had suggested she was a traitor.

"That's okay, Devon. John will finish up here while I go to the ladies' room. Oh, and please stop calling me ma'am."

"Yes, Ms. Saunders."

"April will do," she replied as she opened the hall door. She stepped out but stayed close to the door as she looked up and down the hall. No sign of the reporters. Breathing a sigh of relief, she headed for the restroom.

****

April left John cooling his heels in the Columbia Room while she went for carry-out. No one knew her yet, but he might create some interest. When she returned, she was lugging two bags. One contained two Whoppers, and the other two orders of French fries. "I didn't get drinks since we have water on the bar. It was too much to carry."

"That's fine," John said as he helped her spread out the napkins and unload the food. Once they were settled, John said, "I'm sorry I didn't tell you about Devon's contract. I knew it wasn't an issue, and I just didn't think to say anything."

April had just taken a huge bite out of her Whopper so she couldn't reply right away. She held up her hand to let him know she was busy chewing. He nodded and took a bite out of his own. She turned her head slightly to get a better view while she chewed. *God, he's a handsome man,* she thought. His hair didn't even look real. It was full and perfectly coiffed though she didn't think he went to that much trouble. It just seemed to know where to go. The white strands laced through the raven black of the others created a perfect balance. His profile was strong — firm, but responsive features — and those eyes! She had never seen smoky gray eyes before. They were enhanced by the darkness of his hair, lending a distinguished air to him.

"How old are you?" she asked after she swallowed. She cringed. She hadn't meant to say that aloud. "I'm sorry. That was rather rude."

"It's okay. I don't mind," John replied. "I'm forty years old." Grinning, he added, "I know — I don't look a day over thirty-two."

April laughed. *Actually he doesn't*, she thought.

Deciding to let John's misstep on the contract go, April finished up her Whopper and fries without commenting on it. Glancing at her watch, she realized it was ten minutes till four. She just had time to freshen up before Laney Whitcombe arrived. "Excuse me, John, but I'm going to check my lipstick before Laney shows up. Do you mind waiting here in case she arrives early? I'll hurry in case you need to go to the men's room."

"No problem," John replied as he raked the debris from lunch into the trash can. Giving him a little wave, April left.

Looking around, John wondered what had led him to this place in time. He hadn't been unhappy with Nora or with Oliver & Company. Of course, he knew she had been unhappy with his inability to produce a new work, but he didn't think she would have kicked him to the curb. He was certain he would have slipped down her priority ladder a few rungs. If April hadn't taken his hand and led him down this path, well, he wasn't sure where he'd have been in six months. At least now he had the chance of a brighter path.

There was something about April. He had fallen victim to it that first day at lunch. He had stayed away for a while, trying to regain his objectivity, but he had failed. His one concession to his pride at this point was suppressing his emotions until he saw something to tell him it wasn't a unilateral affair between them. There was a lot at stake. He had burned the bridge behind him professionally so there was no turning back. His future depended on Center Stage Press and April. He couldn't jeopardize this no matter how he felt about her. If he showed his hand too soon, she might react adversely and choose to downplay his books in the future, causing them to quickly become backlist titles. Backlist titles sold but were not bestsellers and represented a much smaller portion of the sales for the industry. Since all his future books belonged to her, he would have to step carefully romantically if he wanted his professional career to survive.

While waiting for April to return and Laney to arrive, John flipped through Devon's contract, which April had left on top of her briefcase. He knew the percentage clauses would be different than his, but he assumed the rest would be standard until he reached the item stipulating the length of the contract.

He quickly read: *The conditions of this contract shall be determined by April Saunders, the representative of Center Stage Press, for a period of fifteen years. During this time, any decision by said party to terminate will be based on performance by the author. Contribution to the evaluation of said author's performance in regard to any decision by Center Stage Press or its representative to terminate this contract shall include, but not be limited to, the following: The author's sales (including the stipulations noted in the Royalties section of this contract), production of works on a timely basis as required by the publisher, and marketing efforts for all books under this contract. After the fifteen year period, termination of the contract may be made by either party without explanation.*

John was stunned. She had left Devon an out. He, on the other hand, had been shackled to her for life! A warmth crept up his body from his toes until he could feel the heat in his cheeks as he struggled to contain his rage. A slight tilting of his vantage point, however, cooled his ire quickly. *What if it meant she didn't want to take a chance on losing him? What if she were paving the way for them to be in this together for the long haul?* He couldn't help smiling. Maybe it wasn't a one-sided affair at all.

April returned to see a lopsided grin on John's face. Puzzled, she asked, "A bestseller for *your* thoughts this time."

Shaken from his reverie, John laughed. "Just musing. Nothing worth putting into words."

A knock on the door disturbed their conversation. John went to open the door. "Laney! I'm so glad you came!"

Stepping into the room to let the door close behind her, she remarked, "Well, of course, I came. Do you think I'd pass up an opportunity to meet with you? Besides, you were just secretive enough to arouse my curiosity — and you know about me and my curiosity! Well, of course, you do. That was the point, was it not?"

John laughed, "If I weren't too young for you, I'd marry you in a minute, Laney. You have such a total disregard for social conventions. No beating around the bush for you." Turning, he thrust his arm in the direction of April. "Laney, this is April Saunders, and I think she has an offer to make you that will curl your hair."

Laney reached up to pat her hair. "I've grown rather fond of the pixie look, but I'm open to a little Shirley Temple." John laughed as Laney reached out and gripped April's hand in a firm grip.

Pulling out a chair, Laney dropped into it. April wondered what it was about this woman that appealed to her. She was bold and saucy, which April doubted was connected to her age. She was not thin, but her clothes seemed to accentuate every positive aspect of her body. Her hair was mostly white and slightly spiky. If April had to guess, she would say Laney was about fifty-five years old; however, her guess was more influenced by her hair color and what she knew of her history. To April's delight, Laney had the unexpected enthusiasm of someone less battered by life.

April and John sat across from Laney, but before either could speak, Laney took charge. "Well, April, spit out your offer so we can see if we need to haggle or call it quits."

Even aware of her boldness, April was taken aback by her statement. Straightening her shoulders, she intuitively knew it was important to meet this woman on equal ground if she ever intended to be in charge. "Well, Laney, before I 'spit out my offer,' I'd like you to tell me why — other than your curiosity —you took the chance of meeting with us today. What is it you want?"

Laney smiled and looked at John. "Well now, a spirited female. I like that." Looking back at April, she said, "I'm looking for a new stable. My publisher is stuck in the past and trying to keep me trapped there with him."

April waited for her to continue. Clearing her throat, Laney proceeded. "I started writing romance novels when I was young and romantic. I was good at it, too. I even enjoyed it for a few decades, but now my life is different. I'm different. Romance novels no longer appeal to me. My libido is no longer crowding out my mental inquisitiveness. I want to write something that doesn't bore me to death. I want to write mysteries or thrillers. Life is complicated and messy. Few things turn out the way we want, despite our best efforts. So I want to write something that reflects life and who I am today, not who I was in my twenties and thirties." Laney locked her gaze on April as if daring her to question her reasons.

"I agree," replied April. "I think a writer has to reach within to pull the best out of themselves. If you just keep trying to follow someone else's formula, you'll never truly express yourself. I mean, you probably were expressing yourself in the beginning, right?" Laney nodded. "The problem is that the natural course of life moves you beyond flighty, romantic experiences, even beyond the ever-popular heart palpitations. Other issues move to the forefront. If you feel the pull of these things in your life, you should be able to express them through whatever genre feels the most compatible."

Laney was silent for a moment before turning once again to John. "Where in hell did you find this woman? I've been looking everywhere for someone who had some common sense mixed in with their business sense." John chuckled at her remark, knowing she was already onboard. "Well, April, let's talk turkey here. I like what you're saying so let's find out if I like what you've put down on paper."

April whipped out the contract. "I think you'll find everything to your liking. If not, I'm sure you'll let me know," April said, a smile lifting the left corner of her mouth.

Taking the contract, Laney spoke as April and John started to rise. "Just wait here. I'm a speed reader. No point in your wasting time making yourselves invisible." They both sat back down and watched as she sped through the contract.

Clearing her throat, Laney looked first at John and then let her gaze settle on April. "I think I'm going to like being with Center Stage Press. One thing, though: you do realize I'll be giving John here a run for his money."

Startled by the comment, John said, "What do you mean? It'll take you a while to get that sticky sweetness off your keyboard from all those romance novels."

Laughing, she replied, "Under all that sticky sweetness is a brazen hussy, John. You should know that. You better step back because the real me is about to burst forth!"

April watched the two of them bantering with each other. It

actually felt good to be part of something where people weren't so competitive with each other, so willing to step on anyone to get what they wanted even though April knew this has been her modus operandi in every job she'd ever had. It hadn't bothered her, though, because she'd always felt her survival depended on her making the first move and having the last word. Maybe things were changing. Maybe.

Chapter 14

Nora Oliver slid her card through the security lock for the elevators. It was only five o'clock in the morning. Other than the doorman, she was probably the only one in the building. The elevators weren't unlocked until seven o'clock. As the elevator rose to the floor occupied by Oliver & Company, Nora thought about how many years she had been riding this elevator, how many years Oliver & Company had been producing the oxygen she breathed. She couldn't even remember doing anything else. There was a time, when Donald was alive, she had been able to breathe somewhere other than here. Now, she felt alone and invisible when she was anywhere but in these offices.

The elevator doors opened, and Nora stepped out into the reception area of her company. Looking around, she was filled with a sense of dread. Things were not going well. She had lost her premier author, John Blackridge, and then her newest success, Devon McNally, had jumped ship soon after. Of course, she was still getting the revenue from their published books, but she was going to have to revamp her budget all the same. There would be no more bestsellers from them.

Last night she had gone out for a drink at the hotel bar next to her condo high-rise. Being alone, she had sat at the end of the bar. As she nursed her drink, she heard a conversation from somewhere behind her. They were speculating on how long it would be before Oliver & Company went belly-up. Shock had coursed through her veins, and a tingling sensation lingered from her head to her toes. Her hand shook, and the drink sloshed on the counter. It was like an omen. Some stranger had voiced the dread which had been in her heart. She had quickly tossed money on the bar and left.

As she stood in the reception area this morning, she could almost hear the crumbling taking place within the walls. There was a hollowness in the air which had nothing to do with her being the only one here. If she listened hard enough, she wondered if she would hear the death knell. She jumped as the elevator bell dinged. Placing her hand on her heart, she chuckled, realizing how melodramatic she was being. Still, a dread enveloped her so tightly she was barely able to hold panic at bay.

With her head down and digging in her purse, Jean Wilson stepped off the elevator and almost collided with Nora. "Sorry! I didn't know anyone was here."

Nora smiled. Jean was the hardest working of her editors and also the most cantankerous. She had been with Nora since the beginning, and Nora loved her for it. "I thought I'd get an early start this morning. What are you doing here so early?" Nora asked.

"Oh, I'm trying to edit that book by Oscar Greene. He has a great story, but he has a tendency to use five words when he could have used two."

"Not one of those!" Nora laughed. It was a pet peeve of every editor because it showed the author's lack of confidence in his writing. Why say "it seemed, as he thought about it, that it was possible" when you could easily say "he now thought it was possible"? No point in beating around the bush.

As Nora parted ways with Jean and walked into her office, she realized how good it had felt to laugh. How long had it been? Just before Blackridge dropped his bomb? She had overreacted. She knew this, but his announcement had been the proverbial straw. She had been informed just a few days earlier that their revenue was down for the current fiscal year. If nothing changed, her accountant told her, she would have to cut back. She had fretted over the situation and finally figured out a way to hold things together with the current revenues, at least until they were able to get more books into the marketplace. Then Blackridge had happened, followed by McNally. If the bar talk was any indication, the stink of failure was apparently already wafting through the streets of Chicago. *What next?* she wondered.

The real reason she had come in early today was because she had a decision to make. She had managed to hold the axe steady for nearly a month, but now there was nothing else she could do. Someone would have to go, maybe even two. She had agonized over her choice, but knew it was the only fair thing to do. April had not been with the company as long as the others. Her salary wouldn't help reduce expenses that much, but Nora was still hoping for a miracle, and she would rather lose April than those who had been with her for years. The others would all have to help out by taking turns manning the phones. She was certain there would be some grumbling, but it couldn't be helped. She would tell April this morning and give her two weeks' severance. She would leave it up to her whether she worked the two weeks or not. It was the least she could do.

The telephone rang, jarring her nerves. Snatching it off the charger, she answered, "Oliver & Company, Nora Oliver."

"Hey, girl! Been a long time." Nora instantly recognized her long-time friend Abby Dickson.

"Hey, yourself! Where have you been? What's it been...six months since we talked last?"

"Something like that. I've been in New York the last three months."

"New York! Why didn't you tell me? What's going on?" she asked, delighted to hear from Abby.

"Oh, everything's great with me. I just signed a contract to illustrate a new series of books for children." Abby was an illustrator, who had been in the business as long as Nora. Abby had illustrated the first children's book she had published.

"Want to go to lunch today?" Nora asked, anxious for a reprieve from work.

"I'd love to, Nora, but I have to meet a budding artist at lunch. He wants to intern with me."

"What? You've never used an intern before."

"I know, but you have to move along with the times, you know. It seems to be the thing to do these days. That way you can shuffle off some of the routine stuff on them, making it possible to take on more projects. Anyway, I would like to meet for lunch maybe later this week—"

"That would be great!" Nora exclaimed.

"In the meantime," Abby continued, "I just thought I'd share some scuttlebutt I heard while in New York. Guess who just left their New York publisher?"

Nora's heart skipped a beat. Weird that yet another author had bailed on their publisher. Of course, Nora wasn't in the same ballpark as the New York publishers, but she was a shining star among the small presses. "I have no idea," she replied.

"Laney Whitcombe!"

"Are you kidding? She's been with the same publisher since before Oliver & Company even existed!"

"I know! Bizarre, isn't it? I wonder what she's planning. I also heard she put her New York apartment on the market. Apparently, she's moving back to Chicago permanently."

There was a slight pause as Nora's mind fixated on the word *planning*. Maybe there was a connection between all these recreants. "That is strange," she agreed. "Be sure to call me about lunch."

"I will. See ya," replied Abby before hanging up.

Nora sat quietly, listening to the soft clacking of Jean's keyboard. Was it possible the desertion of John and Devon was connected to Laney's decision to leave her long-time publisher? Under normal circumstances, she might not have considered the possibility, but if Laney was moving to Chicago permanently, it had to mean that she had a deal here. Nora was pretty sure the small presses headquartered here in Chicago would not be involved. They had all known each other for years and would not likely be trying to undermine the others. Of course, there had been an occasional incident when an author switched houses, but it had always proven to be author-instigated. Still…three at one time?

Chapter 15

The whole condo shook when April slammed the front door. She threw her purse at the sofa and dropped into the armchair, letting her arms and legs splay like a rag doll's. She could not believe what had just happened. Nora had fired her! Technically, she had been laid off, but the end result was the same. Two weeks' severance. *Great!* she thought sarcastically. *How generous.*

After a few more minutes of fuming and filling the air with expletives, April took a deep breath and exhaled very slowly. This was silly. She had been living off her salary, more or less, from Oliver & Company so she still had enough money put aside to last her at least another two years. That was plenty of time to get Center Stage Press underway. She would have to wear a lot of hats, but it could be done.

Glancing at her watch, she picked up the phone to call John. It had been a month since she had signed the contracts with Devon and Laney, and she had left John alone to work on his novel. Devon and Laney both had novels in the works and had promised to have the first draft ready within six months. If she was going to survive ... no she couldn't think like this. She had to survive so she was going to need John's manuscript as soon as possible. She needed something in hand to get investors. She wasn't sure where or how she was going to find them, but she would think of something.

"Hello?" John sounded like he'd been asleep.

"Did I wake you?" she asked, checking her watch to make sure she'd read it correctly. It was only six-thirty.

"Huh? Oh, no, Just caught up in my writing. What's going on?"

"Well, a few things have changed. Nora fired me today—"

"What!" John sat up, releasing his connection to his writing and focusing his thoughts on the phone call. "Did she find out?" His heart was thumping. He knew that Nora was a formidable opponent if she knew what she was fighting.

"No. At least I don't think so. What she told me was that she was having some financial setbacks, and I was lowest in seniority."

"Whew! Thank God," remarked John.

"Why, John, are you afraid of Nora Oliver?" April was surprised by his reaction.

"Not really. It's just that we need to get off the ground before she finds out what is going on. She's been in this business a long time, April, and she has a lot of clout."

"Funny that you should mention timing because this is why I called." April paused, but John waited for her to continue. "Since I am without an income, we need to push this along faster than I had planned. I'm counting on you to provide me with the asset I need to convince an investor or two to front us the capital we need."

There was silence on the other end. Finally John said, "What do you need?" Despite the urgency of the situation at hand, April was touched by John's loyalty. Of course, his neck was in the same noose as hers, but it mattered to her he hadn't erupted in artistic fury at her.

"How far along are you with your first draft?"

John's attitude shifted noticeably as he talked about his novel. "Much farther than I thought I would be. I actually think I'll have the first draft in another month, six weeks tops."

April was stunned. "Six weeks? But you only started it about six weeks ago."

"I know, but I've never spent so much time actually working on a manuscript before. It's like it has taken over my days and my nights. I think about it no matter what I'm doing. I think it's going to be the best I've ever written," he declared immodestly.

Thrilled by his enthusiasm and his deadline, she said, "Let's celebrate tonight if you can tear yourself away. We'll toast to new beginnings."

"Sounds great! I've been working on the story since early this morning. I need a break anyway. I don't want to be found hunched over my keyboard, emaciated, a victim of my artistic muse."

April's laughter rang through the phone, causing John to wonder how much longer he could play it cool.

Chapter 16

Her financial woes were not behind her, but Nora knew that laying off April had been necessary. She hated doing it because April had been doing such a good job. She had picked up on editing much faster than Nora had expected. If things had gone differently, she would have been a good edition to the editing staff. April had chosen not to work the last two weeks. Nora knew she was pissed, but it was just as well. The women in the office needed to adjust to the new way of doing things. Bitching and moaning had been rampant at first, but when she explained it was this or unemployment, the roar had diminished to the level of a whisper.

Nora had spent a lot of time trying to find out what was going on. Blackridge was not out and about as usual, and there was some gossip he was writing the great American novel. She paid scant attention to this because someone was always writing the great American novel. She gave the rumors a bit of credence, however, simply because he had not shown his handsome countenance at any of the normal functions. Could he be avoiding her? Somehow, she doubted it. Still, if he was writing, where was he expecting to sell it?

Then there was Devon. All she'd found out about him was from a groupie, who was about twenty-one years old. Nora had seen her hanging around for the last couple of years. She wasn't sure what her scheme was, but she had seen her with Devon several times in the past. At the recent gathering of publishers and writers for an awards dinner, she had spotted her on the arm of another young writer. Easing over beside her, she asked innocently, "Have you seen Devon?"

"Not lately. The last time I saw him, he was rather excited though."

"Oh?" Here it comes, thought Nora. "What about?"

"I don't know. All I could get out of him was that 'life is looking up'."

Disappointed, Nora remarked, "Well, I guess that's always a good sign." Smiling, she turned to leave. "Good to see you again."

"You, too," the girl replied before turning a dazzling smile on her escort.

Nora had grabbed a glass of champagne off the waiter's tray as he passed and returned to her table. Sipping slowly, she had tried to put the pieces of information together in some way that made sense. Trouble was, they just didn't. She knew there was something in the wind — if she could only figure out what it was.

****

Having raced from one task to another over the last few weeks, April was taking a break to assess the status of Center Stage Press. Looking down the street from her condo, she could barely see the office building where her new offices would be located. She had managed to get half of the top floor. The current lessee was in jail after only two months into the current year's lease. Times were tough right now for leasing of office space, especially pricey office space. April had convinced the manager to let her rent half of the floor and finish out the ten months on the lease at fifty percent of the pro-rated rent rather than his having it sit empty. Now she had time to get revenue coming in so she could afford the full rent, and meanwhile, the landlord should be able to rent the other half of the floor more easily.

Closing her eyes, April imagined how the sign would look once it arrived. Because the office was on the top floor, she had rights to put her company name on the building. For the color, she had chosen an emerald green because at night, it would stand out, sparkling against the sky like a gem. Knowing the rumor mills would definitely rev up if the name of a new small press showed up on a building near the heart of the city, she decided to wait until her first publication was ready to go. There was no advantage in playing her hand too soon.

Settling back on the couch, her mind automatically began checking off her list of things to do. She had created a detailed spreadsheet to make sure she didn't miss any aspect of the business, but she didn't need to drag it out of her briefcase. She could see the entire sheet in her head. All her business licenses were completed. She had registered and purchased ISBNs to establish her publisher code. She had researched and discovered an incredible webmaster, who held a master's degree in graphic design and in computer technology. What April liked most about her was her flair for creating layouts and designs that were interesting but didn't diminish the impact of the important elements.

April was still investigating book production companies, but she had narrowed it down to two. She knew that a number of small presses were now using print-on-demand companies instead to take the strain off their budget. Perhaps she would in the future, but now she wanted to pattern herself after the Big Six publishers — inventory and all. Maybe one day, it would be the Big Seven publishers. She laughed aloud at the thought. You could never dream too big!

Eventually, she would need to hire editors, but for John's book, she planned to act as his editor. She still needed to hire an advertising agency, not to mention a sales person with a background in the industry, who could work well with the distributors. She made a mental note to set up a meeting with John to discuss a marketing plan. He had been doing this for years and would be able to offer her valuable insights.

Despite the tremendous step she was taking, April wasn't worried. Perhaps it was her cyclothymic mania that was holding her spirits high. Whatever it was, she didn't care. All she knew was that making a success of Center Stage Press was what she wanted, and that was enough.

April's mind slipped effortlessly to thoughts of John. His presence ignited the feeling that a different path was calling to her. It scared her because she couldn't afford to lose her focus. When she was with him, her hard-edged, observant personality morphed without warning into a devil-may-care attitude, which was dangerous. She had to stay in control for both their sakes.

Her mental eye fell on the last item on her list: Get Investors. Not having any collateral had made this the one area where April felt uncertain. Without warning, a name popped into her head — Harmon, the last project Jeffrey Taber had given her. Harmon had supposedly been encroaching on Jeffrey's Village Projects by trying to outbid him on land purchases, a nuisance, but one with the potential of undermining Jeffrey's lucrative plan to dominate the construction industry in this area.

When April left Dietz & Holcombe, she hadn't bothered to return any of the paperwork she had taken home with her for one reason or other. Nor did she empty her briefcase before barreling out of the office that day. She had been so angry when she got home that she'd gathered up everything and thrown it into the hall closet. Now her mind was racing. She could almost taste victory.

She was certain she had a copy of the seven-year-plan Dietz & Holcombe had established for the Village Projects. It had a list of all the properties they intended to purchase. She just needed to do a little research on Harmon Industries to find out the name of the man with the power and the money. She was pretty sure her information was worth at least a million dollars. The Village Projects would rake in billions. Finally, she thought, she had something she could sell. The best part was that she wouldn't have to pay it back or have investors trying to tell her what to do. A simple oversight on Jeffrey's part in not recovering all the company documents from April might well be the answer to her prayers *and* let her taste a little revenge as well.

****

When April had told John about securing the new office space, he was flabbergasted. She never ceased to amaze him by her courage. He didn't consider himself a wuss, but he wasn't sure he had ever stepped off such a high cliff before, at least not without a net. He convinced himself it was her courage in the face of adversity that drove him to make life easier for her. He wasn't quite able yet to admit the hold she had on him.

Even writing this book was a mixture of his own passion for the story and his passion for doing a good job for her. Nearing the end of his first draft, he had been extremely careful, editing as he went, which he rarely did. He knew it would help April if she didn't have to start from scratch with the grammar and punctuation. Despite the poor reputation writers had in this area, he was quite adept at editing. In the past, he had let it fall by the wayside because there were plenty of women in Nora's office to deal with it.

Looking out across Lake Michigan, he wondered what the future held. He had never felt this way about a woman before. He was forty years old and had never even had a long-term relationship beyond six months. Most women he had met bored him after a while. April was never boring. Watching the undulation of the water as it gently rolled toward shore, John wondered if this was the way their relationship would always be. Would it flow gently along, never disturbing the status quo? Or would their passion eventually take hold and churn it up to heights they had never imagined until they broke from the strain of it all?

Tentatively allowing himself to explore his feelings, John realized that the relationship he desired with April was a balance of the heightened passion and the gentle flow. He sensed she was a woman of extremes, both personally and professionally. He found himself wanting to be the one on whom she could depend, the one who balanced her load so she was never overwhelmed. Of course, he acknowledged there was a selfish element to this desire, for his professional career was now permanently entwined with hers. Yet, he was driven by a depth of emotion that centered around being there for her, regardless of his career.

Chapter 17

"Are you traveling for business or pleasure?" asked the young man sitting next to April. His remark drew her out of her thoughts. She had been working out her plan for approaching Derek Harmon. She'd called ahead to make an appointment, but she had only told the secretary it was related to the Village Projects by Dietz & Holcombe, which were apparently the magic words.

"A little of both," she replied to her seatmate. Closing this deal would do more than jumpstart Center Stage Press. It would also give her some closure for the way Jeffrey had treated her. Just the thought of it was orgasmic, giving her much more pleasure than her interludes with Jeffrey.

The young man smiled at her but refrained from continuing the conversation. Perhaps he sensed that her mind was miles away. April hardly noticed as she slipped back into mentally testing out her approach. In her research, she had seen a picture of Derek. He was middle-aged, perhaps forty-five. He was handsome in a rugged sort of way. His hair was a little long and, of course, blonde, the perfect California poster child. It was difficult to decide how to handle Derek without some knowledge of him. Would she need to manipulate him or would her "gift" to him be enough? She chuckled, and the young man next to her smiled tentatively, not sure if it was directed to him.

"Something funny?" he asked.

"Huh? Oh, I guess you could say that," she replied. "Do you know that saying — the worm turns?" she asked, shifting to face him.

"Yeah," he replied eagerly. "We just finished studying it in my Shakespeare class at the university. It was in Shakespeare's Henry VI." He cleared his throat. "Let's see if I can remember. I should, considering how many times we went over it."

Before April could stop him, he began to recite, "To whom do lions cast their gentle looks? Not to the beast that would usurp their den. Whose hand is that the forest bear doth lick? Not his that spoils her young before her face. Who 'scapes the lurking serpent's mortal sting?

Not he that sets his foot upon her back. The smallest worm will turn being trodden on, And doves will peck in safeguard of their brood." He smiled proudly at April.

"That's wonderful!" she cried. "I had no idea that's where it originated." As she thought about what he said, it seemed to fit the circumstances perfectly. Jeffrey had trod upon her, and now she was turning. The resemblance of Jeffrey's actions to her own with Brandon Foster never crossed her mind.

Harmon Industries had its own high-rise building in Los Angeles with incredible landscaping. Despite the monolith rising from its center, the grounds incorporated trees, plants, waterfalls, and cobblestone walks in an area that circled the building, radiating out at least five hundred feet. The trees were large enough to provide shade for the walkways. April could hear the sounds of waterfalls from both directions as she travelled the main path to the entrance. When she reached a cobblestone path that branched off, she could see a park bench about fifteen feet away, surrounded by an array of flowers in every color imaginable.

Glancing at her watch, she decided to take a minute to enjoy this oasis in the city. Sitting down on the bench, she looked up toward the sky. All she could see were the branches of the tree shading this area. Between them she saw fragments of the windows on the upper floors of the building. She imagined the ends of the branches reaching out like fingers to make contact with the strange monument in its midst. She was taken aback by how much effort must have gone into creating this incredible garden. Apparently, there was more to this Harmon fellow than she had thought. Another quick glance at her watch told her it was time. She brushed off her skirt and headed toward the entrance.

"Is it *Ms* Saunders?" Derek Harmon inquired as he directed her toward the chair in front of his desk.

"Yes, but you may call me April."

"Fine. April, it is." Derek sat down, tilting his chair back. "I must admit I'm intrigued by what you told my secretary when you made your appointment. She said you had some information regarding the Village Projects by Dietz & Holcombe that I would be *very* interested in hearing. My secretary even underlined the word *very*." April simply nodded. She did not want to jump right into her spiel. Let him ask her for the information first. "So," he continued, "before we get started, would you like something to drink?"

"Yes, I would love something to drink. The taxi ride from the airport took longer than I thought, and I didn't get a chance to stop for lunch."

"Airport? Did you fly in for this appointment?" Derek was surprised. He hadn't really expected anything from this meeting, figured she was some secretary at one of Dietz & Holcombe's projects in California. The secretary had failed to get a return number.

"Yes," she replied. "I flew in from Chicago." April noticed how he straightened up in his chair. She could feel the line tightening as her prey took the bait.

Punching the intercom button, he said, "Susan, reschedule my next appointment. April, uh … Ms. Saunders hasn't had lunch so we will be out for a while." Turning to April, he asked, "Is that all right with you?"

Laughing, she replied, "Are you kidding? Right now, I would kill for food!"

Smiling, he walked around his desk and took her arm. "It will be much easier to talk on a full stomach, and I suspect we have something *very* interesting to talk about."

Derek carefully avoided the purpose of her visit on the way to the restaurant, and April let him control the situation for now. Once they ordered, Derek leaned to one side, placing his elbow on the table and two of his fingers under his chin. "So, April, what is this information that I'm going to be interested in hearing about?" Before she could answer, he said, "I have a feeling that it's going to cost me." He held her gaze, and a corner of his mouth angled upward. April recognized the move. She had used it herself many times. She chuckled. Perhaps there was more to be had here than just a million dollars, she thought, but quickly reined herself back in. She had already been down that road. Besides, she had her own business to consider now.

Smiling at him, April said, "Yes, it is going to cost you, but you'll be able to reap billions from this information."

Derek was unable to keep from reacting to her bold statement. He had thought this would be an interesting little jaunt with an incredibly beautiful woman, after which he would let her down gently. Even when he discovered she was from Chicago, the headquarters for Dietz & Holcombe, he had doubted her information was anything important. How much valuable information could a secretary get her hands on — especially information worth billions?

"By the look on your face, I believe you have underestimated me. Are you asking yourself how a secretary could possibly have such valuable information?" she asked.

All his diplomatic skills failed him as his mouth gaped open. "Uh…"

"No need to apologize. You're just doing what most people do. Just so you understand the game, I was a Vice-President at Dietz & Holcombe until about a year ago—"

"Hey, listen. I apologize for my prejudice. It was completely out of line," he stuttered. The last thing he wanted to do was insult her before he found out what she was selling.

"That's not a problem. I'm a big girl. I can handle it. Are you ready to hear what I have to offer you?"

"Absolutely," he replied quickly, placing both elbows on the table and leaning forward.

"I understand that you've been bidding against Jeffrey Taber on properties he wants to use for his Village Projects. Is that correct?" Derek nodded. "How would you like to know which properties he has lined up to purchase to support his seven-year plan?"

Derek could barely breathe. If he knew this, he could purchase all the properties before Taber even knew what hit him. It would ensure the dominance of Harmon Industries in this new arena. "You actually have this?" April nodded and waited for him to continue. "How do you know it's still valid info?"

"I know because I was there when it was researched and proposed. These properties are the top properties in the country. Jeffrey's waiting for revenues from the early projects to start coming in before taking the leap. He has three active projects at the moment, and according to his plan, it will be at least ten to twelve months before he begins the purchasing of new properties."

Scratching his head, Derek asked, "How does he know they will be available then?"

"Well, Jeffrey's a pretty clever guy. All these properties are in the path of growth, but because they're such large parcels and still just beyond the growth path, no one is beating a path to the door of the owners. When a project is two years out, his plan is to notify the property owner that he has the intention of purchasing their property for a large sum of money in less than two years. His offer will be much more than they could be sure of receiving if they sold the land off piecemeal."

"How many properties are there?"

"Twenty minus the three that he has already started."

Derek was quiet for a few minutes. April did not interrupt his thoughts. Finally, he said, "How much do you want for this information?"

"I want two things. First, the details of the transaction must be confidential. I don't want to find myself being sued by Jeffrey. Second, I want one million dollars wired to my bank account before I leave."

Derek was not fazed by the amount. He understood the value of what she was offering him. "I will have to check them out before I transfer any money."

"I will give you the names of two of them, and you can check them out. If you're satisfied, we will close the deal." She waited for his answer.

Grinning, Derek said, "This has turned out to be one helluva lunch. You'll need to stay overnight. Can I drive you to a hotel?"

"That would be wonderful. Thank you," April replied. She could feel the tingle of power getting stronger. Mr. Jeffrey Taber was investing in her new business whether he liked it or not. Unfortunately, for him, it was going to be a losing proposition.

Chapter 18

A sigh of relief escaped from April's lips as she looked out across her new offices. The build-out had been less expensive and faster than she'd thought, and the result was incredible. Her private office faced Lake Michigan, sharing the same view as her condo. She had chosen a traditional reception area which she had furnished with plush carpet, a couple of paintings, an elegant desk, and matching chairs for clients. Other than her own office, she had divided part of the remaining square footage into a conference room, a bullpen for the editors and staff, three large offices for her golden circle, and a smaller one for clients to use if necessary, two restrooms, one with a shower, and a break room with some kitchen facilities. All the rooms were furnished well, but she had been careful with the budget.

Looking past the restrooms and the break room, there was a door at the end of the hall. Beyond this door lay a room that took up the end of the office space from one side to the other so it wasn't noticeable to the unaware, and it was only accessible through that one door. To most, the door would appear to be the access to a storage closet. In fact, it was the entrance to a large room, furnished as a bedroom and sitting room. April was covering her bases. If things didn't go well and she should have to leave her condo down the road, she would have a place to live. She was not going to let her personal needs — like a place to sleep — interfere with the success of Center Stage Press. The landlord had no idea how she was using this area, and April had no intention of telling him. It was her sanctuary.

Since Harmon had wired the million dollars into her account, she had been more excited about the future of Center Stage Press than ever. Money was power, and now she had the means to move forward with her plans. The office was just the beginning.

Her phone rang. Before she even pulled the phone out of her purse, she knew it was John. "Hello," she said as she flipped the phone open.

"Good news! The final draft is complete!" April could hear the excitement in his voice.

"Are you kidding? That's wonderful! When can I see it?" she asked, her own excitement matching his.

"How's tonight? We could grab a bite and then go back to your apartment so you can read the first few chapters and tell me what you think. Then I'll leave you to it. How's that sound?"

"Wonderful. Let's meet in front of my apartment and walk to the Lakeside Bistro. Is that okay?" April asked.

John smiled. Comfort food was starting to become a regular with them. "Thirty minutes?"

"I'll be there."

****

Returning home, April pushed her key into the condo's front door lock. She could feel John's presence behind her, the heat radiating off him. Not a sweaty heat, but a musky, gentle warmth that made her want to turn around and pull him into her arms. She wasn't sure how long she could keep her distance. The first hint from him, and she knew she'd be in trouble. The lock clicked, and the door swung open easily. She shed her imaginings and headed into the condo. John followed close behind.

April quickly settled in on the sofa to read the beginning of John's novel. It was exciting for so many reasons: it was the first book for Center Stage Press; it sprang from her own work; and despite her determination to keep her business and personal lives separate, she couldn't deny that knowing John wrote it and that she was the first to read it was exhilarating.

John fixed himself something to drink and chose a chair that allowed him to look at Lake Michigan. Sitting calmly while she read the words that had sprung from his heart, waiting to hear her judgment of it, was excruciating, but he promised himself he would not attempt to persuade her opinion in any way.

Forty-five minutes later, April laid the manuscript on the table and headed for the kitchen. John shifted so that he could watch her. She said nothing until she returned to the sofa with drink in hand. Sitting down, she braced her back against the arm of the sofa and faced him.

"John," she said. He looked at her face, searching for some indication of where this was going. "John, I have read a lot of books, including your earlier ones, and I have to say that I am shocked by what I've read so far." His heart literally fell into his stomach, creating a loud rumbling of discontent, but he managed to maintain a neutral expression.

"I am shocked that you have grown to this level so quickly. Your earlier books were good, but this is in a different category altogether." John released a loud sigh. April laughed. "What? Did you think I didn't like it?"

"Well, it crossed my mind," he replied.

"John, I have no doubt that we have a winner. I knew you could do it. Center Stage is going to burst out of the starting gate and never look back!"

As April spoke, John crossed the room to the sofa and sat down on the edge facing her. He leaned across her and kissed her on the cheek. Pulling back slightly, he grinned but didn't move. A brief moment passed before she put her hands on the sides of his face and pulled him toward her. The passion he could feel radiating off of her catapulted John to a much higher emotional level than her reaction to his novel had. He would never have thought it possible, but this feeling was worth more to him than his novel.

When April pulled back, she saw disappointment flash across his face. For the first time in her life, she was actually concerned about hurting a man. Still, she should make a choice between the business or a relationship with John if the past was any indication. Perhaps this would be different, she thought. She had never actually cared about any of the men in her past. They were simply a means to an end. With John, it was different. He *was* a means to an end, but her feelings for him were more than that. He made her laugh. He made her feel alive. He actually cared about her. Perhaps, this one *was* different, she thought as she stood and reached for his hand.

****

April looked in the mirror which was fogged by the heat from her shower. Slipping her towel from around her, she wiped the mirror clean. Looking at herself, she accepted how desirable she was to men. Of course, this was only the surface April. There was much more than met the eye, and most men missed it. They were too busy ogling her and letting their imaginations run wild. Not John. She had never expected the sex to be more than sex because she had never thought men were capable of any more than that. She was so wrong. John was a great lover, and he had actually talked to her, wondered what she was thinking and how she felt. During one break in the long and glorious evening of lovemaking, he had asked her what her one big desire in life was. She had almost laughed until she realized he was serious.

She had been unable to answer him right away. Of course, she wanted Center Stage Press to succeed, but was that her one big desire in life? Now that he had focused her attention on it, she wasn't sure. To not be taken lightly had popped into her head, but she hadn't spoken the thought aloud. It seemed so shallow. She was not able to answer him truthfully. Instead she had laughed and told him "I'll save that for another time." The truth was, his question was now starting to haunt her. It somehow seemed important to know what her one big desire in life was.

Stepping out of the bathroom, she could see the imprint of John's body on the sheets. He had left an hour ago, but his impression remained on her bed and, she had to admit, in her heart. She dressed quickly because they planned to meet for lunch, and then she wanted to show him their new offices.

Chapter 19

Five months later

The night sky literally sparkled as April walked from her condo to the offices of Center Stage Press. She glanced up and stopped to admire the green glow of the sign announcing to the world that she was a mover-and-shaker. In less than nine months she had taken a dream and not only made it a reality, she had exploded onto the publishing scene. Her memories were punctuated by three glorious moments.

The first was when she had shown John the new offices. They had just had a relaxing lunch. The previous night's lovemaking still lingered in the air. April had never seen a man "glow" before. She had seen it in her own mirror that morning, and sitting across from John, she was certain that there was an aura about him that hadn't been there before, a lightness of spirit.

When they reached the penthouse floor, April had made John cover his eyes as she opened the main door. She pushed him gently through the doorway and closed the door behind her. "You can look now," she'd said.

John had looked around the room. He wasn't surprised by it. He had known she was up to something long before their trip to the penthouse of this office building. He couldn't imagine her doing anything less than shooting for the top. He had pulled her close and squeezed. There was no need to say anything. Her dream, and now his dream as well, was gathering momentum, and they both knew it.

The second glorious moment was when her banner in the sky, announcing that she had laid claim to the top of the world, lit up for the first time. The words Center Stage Press had glowed with a subtle air of superiority, sharing their green aura with those below. April had read once that people with green auras were very successful business people, creating a great deal of wealth and prosperity for themselves because they were meticulous, rarely making rash decisions. There was no doubt in her mind that green was the perfect color for her.

Her one wish that night had been that she could be a fly on the wall when Nora Oliver heard about Center Stage and when she saw the sign. True, it wasn't as reserved as Oliver & Company's snobbishly underplayed brass plaque, but it reflected the spirit of Center Stage Press and its owner to a T.

The third glorious moment was when John's novel was launched. There had been shock waves in the publishing world. The first shock was the discovery that a bestselling author like John Blackridge had aligned himself with a fledgling publishing company. The second shock was the level of marketing the "inexperienced Ms. Saunders," as April was often described, had managed to produce. The third shock was when John's book hit the bestseller lists practically before it hit the shelves.

April smiled as she headed into the elevator and punched the penthouse button. Laney and Devon were neck-to-neck in their race to see whose book was chosen to be the next one out of the gate. Of course, April had already decided that it would be Devon. Laney would probably not understand at first, but it was all about timing. Since Devon was a new author, albeit a bestselling one, he was not the powerhouse that Laney was. April was certain that Devon's book would be a bestseller, but readers were not as familiar with him. While marketing his release, she would be teasing readers with Laney's upcoming release in a new genre. She knew there was a risk of losing Laney's die-hard romance fans, but if they played their cards right with the marketing, curiosity would bring them in, and Laney's skills as a writer would keep them there.

The elevator doors slid open and April stepped out into the hallway. Her heart skipped a beat when she saw someone standing there. Quickly recognizing Devon, she curtly asked, "Been hanging around long?" He was not supposed to come to the office until his book release was announced.

Unabashedly, Devon shook his head. "I assumed you'd come by here after dinner so I thought I'd wait."

"Am I that predictable?" she asked as she reached into her purse for the office keys.

"Pretty much," Devon replied, not realizing that his response could qualify as an insult of sorts to April.

"Well, I'll have to see what I can do about that," she remarked. Devon still had that tendency of the young to speak the truth without regard to the consequences. She accepted his remark as a heads-up. Becoming predictable was how you made yourself vulnerable.

Opening the door, she walked toward her office. Devon followed, carrying a box-style briefcase. "What's so urgent that it couldn't wait until we could meet elsewhere?"

Ignoring the implications of her remark, Devon plopped down on the first chair he came to inside her office. "I've finished my book," he stated.

"And?" April couldn't help but torment him a little after his remark in the hall.

"And I wanted to get it to you before Laney," he said, his facial expression indicating that he was questioning her sanity. "I want my book launched next," he declared with feigned bravado.

Turning to face him, she placed her purse on the desk. "Now, Devon, I know that you and Laney have each been engaged in this imaginary race to finish your novel first, but you didn't really think that it was an actual race, did you?" The look on his face answered her question.

"I have a plan, Devon, and it doesn't involve a race to the finish line for either of you. If you are comfortable with your manuscript, I'll certainly take it and start reading it. As soon as I get Laney's manuscript in my hands and have read it as well, I will meet with the both of you and John to let you know of my plans.

"In the meantime, I want you to be working on a marketing plan that will get you in front of as many people as you can once we start the publicity. I'd like to have this in my hands in two weeks. Can you do that?"

All the wind taken out of his sails, Devon simply nodded. He knew he was still a newcomer to the industry, despite his initial success, but he also knew that he had a good deal going with Center Stage Press. Besides, he was no match for Ms. Saunders. Handing her the manuscript, he turned and left without a word.

Not able to settle the thoughts that had been whirling around in his head all day, Devon pushed through the front door of the building with the intention of walking to John's condo and confronting him to see if he knew what was going on. He took a quick left toward the beach.

Nora Oliver was walking toward the beach from the bar around the corner, trying to clear her head, when she saw Devon. She started to call out, but thrust her hand over her mouth when she realized that he had just emerged from the building housing Center Stage Press.

Oh, my God! she thought. That can't be a coincidence. Why else would he be coming out of that building at this time of night? The pieces started to fall into place. When the sign had appeared on the building, scuttlebutt made its way to her that it had been leased by April Saunders. She and Abby had had a good laugh, trying to imagine what kind of authors she would be able to attract with no background in the business. She had admired her chutzpah but knew there was no chance in hell of her survival.

When the release of John Blackridge's new novel was announced and she saw that it was Center Stage Press, Nora had called Abby immediately. They had met at what was becoming Nora's regular bar. She hadn't known whether to be livid or worried. It didn't seem possible that April could survive with only one author. She was having trouble surviving with the ones she had, and she had been in the business for decades. After a few drinks, she had passed it off to a wild adventure by April and John that would end in disaster. Now, she wasn't so sure.

****

Having worked himself up again, Devon knocked loudly on John's front door.

"Hold your horses!" John called out. "I'm coming!" He threw open the door, ready to take his visitor down a notch or two. Before he could utter a word, Devon rushed past him only to stop dead once he stepped into the living area. Laney Whitcombe was lounging at the end of the sofa with a drink in her hand.

"Cheers, Devon!" she said, raising her glass to him.

Devon whirled around to face John. "What the hell's going on here?" he asked. "Are the two of you scheming against me?"

John frowned, wondering what had Devon so upset. He gently, but persuasively, led Devon toward the sofa. Once he was seated, John asked, "First of all, Devon, I have no idea what we would be scheming about. Obviously, you're upset about something to do with April and Center Stage." Devon started to speak, but John interrupted. "Just so you know, Laney and I would never scheme against you. There's no upside in it, and it's not who we are."

Unable to contain himself, Devon blurted out, "I just went by the office and talked to April—"

"You did what?!" both Laney and John shouted.

"Don't panic. It was dark, and I didn't see anybody."

"Dammit, Devon! You know you're not supposed to be seen with her until your book is ready to be released. What the hell were you thinking?"

"I was thinking that I needed to get my manuscript to her before Laney did if I didn't want to wind up on the short end of the stick. That's what!"

John took a deep breath. Laney just shook her head.

"What?" Devon asked. "It's not like she has a lot of experience in this industry—"

"And you do?" Laney remarked sarcastically.

Chagrined, Devon replied, "Okay, maybe I don't, but what makes you think she knows anything about business?"

John had not intended to reveal what he knew about April, but it was starting to look like he didn't have a choice. "Look, I know you think of April as Nora's receptionist, but what you don't know is that she was the vice-president of one of the largest construction companies in the country a couple of years ago. She got caught in a triangle and lost."

"She told you that?" asked Laney, intrigued, but surprised that the April she knew would divulge such information.

"No. I did some checking on my own before I signed with her. Otherwise, I would have taken my chances with Nora, and I would never have gotten the two of you involved if I didn't believe she is one savvy woman."

"I have to say that I liked her spirit right off, and it didn't hurt that she supported my desires." Laney raised her glass in salute.

"I'm still not sure," Devon groused. "I mean, you two have established reputations, but some people are still expecting me to be a one-book wonder."

"I may be dense after three drinks," interjected Laney, "but I don't see your problem. You're going to be published, and it's up to you if you're a one-book wonder or not."

Devon did not respond to reason that quickly. "The problem is that if she publishes your book next, when my book comes out, I'll look like the best she could do after corralling two powerhouses like you!" he replied petulantly.

"You need to have more faith in yourself, Devon," declared John. "April is not going to give you the short end of the stick, if for no other reason than it wouldn't suit her goals either. Trust me. Whatever she has planned, it is well-thought-out and will use our assets to promote us *and* Center Stage.

"Remember, she has as much, no, really more to lose than any of us. If everything falls apart, it might take a little time and effort, but we would still be writers, and someone would take a chance on us because we have shown our ability to draw an audience. April, however, will be left with nothing except the want ads."

"But—" Devon said.

"I know what you're going to say, Devon, but Laney and I would never leave you out in the cold. We're all in this together. Isn't that right, Laney?"

Seeing that Devon was tearing up, whether out of happiness or misery she didn't know, Laney said, "Devon, sweetie, you need to relax. There's a time to consider your assets and a time to bemoan your liabilities. Right now, you need to shed your angst and count your lucky stars. You have us, and whether you think so or not, I believe you have April. You are in the inner circle of an up-and-coming press. What new author can say that? Plus, no one can ever take away your talent." Pausing, she could tell his angst was slipping away. "Care for a drink?" Devon nodded.

Breathing a sigh of relief, John headed for the bar.

Chapter 20

At The Crossroads Restaurant

Tears rolled down April's cheeks. Grace waved her hand in the air, and April roused from her trance enough to remember where she was. She reached out for her tea glass and took a big swallow. Wiping her hand across the tear tracks on her face, she stared at the water on her hand as if she had never seen anything like it before.

Grace watched as April tried to regain her composure. She knew that letting her emotions flow freely was not comfortable for April. "May I ask why you're crying, dear?" Grace knew, of course, but felt it would be beneficial for April to voice the reason aloud.

"I-I'm not sure," she replied, still staring at her hand.

"Of course you are, dear. You just need to embrace the feelings you're having so you can put them into words."

April looked up from her hand to stare at Grace with the same confused expression. Her thoughts drifted back to the conversation she had just witnessed between John and Devon and Laney. It felt so weird to see not just her past, but the past that paralleled her own, the past of those whose lives she had influenced.

Grace verbally nudged her. "So, what caused those tears to flow so freely?"

Before she could stop them, tears erupted once again. Between sobs, April said, "I never knew John supported me that much. I never knew." Memories of words she had later spat at him made her cringe.

"What about Laney and Devon? They risked everything to sign with you."

Hiccupping, April replied, "I realize that now. I never thought about it before. I was just focused on the success of Center Stage." Pausing, she added reluctantly, "They were just a means to that end." She dropped her head in shame, perhaps for the first time in her life.

Grace waved her hand in the air once again, and April was

transported back in time on a journey not of her choosing.

Chapter 21

Despite the success of John's new book, *Crossing the Rubicon*, April had refused to reveal who the other authors in her stable were. Nora Oliver's friend Abby Dickson had failed to come through for her. However, in that moment of serendipity when Nora saw Devon coming out of the Center Stage Press building, she understood. April had raided her stable of authors. Were there going to be others? After losing her biggest revenue producers, Oliver & Company might not survive the loss of any others. Nora rued the day she had given April a chance. She should have known she would never be satisfied with anything less than the power she had already tasted in her past. With a shudder, Nora realized she was lucky April had chosen to start her own company rather than steal hers. Still, Oliver & Company was definitely wounded, and Nora wasn't sure it was going to live.

****

Devon's unscheduled visit to the office the night before was causing April concern, How much longer could she keep things under wraps? She had spent the entire night reading Devon's manuscript. Much to her surprise, it was delightful! To be so impulsive in his day-to-day responses, she would never have expected such insights in his writing, such complex characters. He even knew how to punctuate!

The next thing on her agenda was to touch base with Laney to find out the status of her manuscript. Picking up the phone, she dialed the number.

"Hello," Laney said, a lilt in her voice.

"Hi, Laney, this is April."

"What perfect timing!" she said. "I was just going to call you. I finished my manuscript this morning. I've been done for days except for the last chapter. Then last night, I woke up and knew what to write." She didn't even pause for breath. "Do you want me to courier it to you? I know you prefer reading paper manuscripts."

Pleased to hear Laney's news, April knew the time had come. She could get everything ready to go. "No, I want all three of you to meet me at the office at four o'clock."

"In the daylight?" Laney inquired, quite aware of her rule about non-disclosure, which included visiting the office. *Had something happened?*

Laughing, April replied, "Yes, in the daylight. We're getting ready to launch our assault on the publishing industry!

"On second thought, Laney, go ahead and messenger your manuscript. I'll read it before you all arrive. See you then!" April hung up.

Her plan was moving along just as she planned. Since she wasn't going to release Laney's book right away, she could focus her attention on the production of Devon's. She would still need to get the ball rolling on Laney's cover. She would need it for the teaser campaign she had planned to prepare people for Laney's genre shift. Clapping her hands in anticipation, she logged into her computer.

At four o'clock, Laney, Devon, and John arrived together. Maria, the receptionist April had hired a few days earlier, looked rather surprised to see them. Up until that moment, no one had entered the offices other than April. Having wondered if accepting the position had been a mistake, she considered it a good sign to see other human beings.

April walked up behind Maria. "Maria, I'd like you to meet John Blackridge." John nodded as Maria gasped. She had read all his books. "This is Devon McNally, the newest shining star in the publishing world." A big smile crossed Maria's face. She had read *The Triumph of the Fates* and loved it. He was even better-looking in person!

Finally, April said, "And this is Laney Whitcombe."

"Oh, my God! Not *the* Laney Whitcombe? I've read all your books since I was a little girl. I used to sneak them out of my mother's room to read them."

Laney laughed. "Keep this up, and you're going to make me think it's time to retire."

"Oh no, don't ever do that! You are such a good writer!"

Laney couldn't resist asking, "Would you read my next book if it was a mystery?"

"I would read it if it was science fiction!"

Laney turned to April. "I'd say that's a good sign!"

Laughing, April led the way to the conference room. Once they were all settled, she revealed her plan for the launching of the second and third books from Center Stage Press. Devon, needless to say, was thrilled. He even apologized for doubting her.

"This will be a busy six months for all of us. John's book is doing great, and my sources tell me that there is much anticipation about what Center Stage will be launching next," she grinned widely, "and we don't want to disappoint.

"Devon, did you bring the marketing ideas we talked about?"

"Yeah," he said as he rummaged in his briefcase.

"Laney, you'll need to do the same thing. Your publicity campaign will be a bit different than Devon's or John's because you're shifting genres. We're going to have to get their interest up about the mystery and let them know that it is not devoid of romance. By the way, I noticed that you have two titles on the manuscript. Which is your favorite? I want to see if we agree."

Despite her veteran status, Laney was nervous. Titling a romance was different than with a mystery. *Fractured Mind* or *Echoes of Terror*? Clearing her throat, Laney said, "I'm not used to mystery titles, but I believe *Fractured Mind* is the best title."

"I agree," replied April. Looking around, she said, "Does everyone have enough information to get started? We'll meet again in a few days. By the way, you each have offices where you can work every day."

They all looked at each other before rushing for the door to pick out the one they wanted. April couldn't help but laugh when she saw that John was the second one out the door. *He's such a kid sometimes,* she thought. It wasn't a putdown. She actually enjoyed his antics. They reminded her of the silliness and the freedom of being a child. It had been a long time since she had felt that carefree.

At first she had been worried he would be clingy or feel entitled, but he had not changed at all. He was the same man she knew before they became intimate. She had never known a relationship with a man that had no strings attached. She hadn't even thought it was possible, but for John, it seemed to be. She knew she had strings in the relationship. She wouldn't tolerate his expecting to be treated differently than her other authors, nor would she countenance his taking the initiative concerning Center Stage without discussing it with her first. As long as he played by the rules, she was thoroughly enjoying their relationship, especially since she was the one in the position to hire and fire this time.

Hiring and firing reminded her that she had an appointment at five-thirty with a potential editor. She had posted an ad in yesterday's paper, but so far she had only received one email response. The woman had asked if she could bring her resume with her instead of emailing it. A little strange, April had thought at the time, but since she was the only responder, she agreed.

The phone in the conference room buzzed. Punching the in-house line, she said, "Yes?"

"There's a woman at the reception desk who says she has an appointment with you at five-thirty. She apologized for being early."

Early is good, thought April. "I'll meet her in reception in just one minute," she replied before clicking off. She closed all her files and set them aside before heading to the front. As she stepped into the reception area, her mouth dropped open. There stood Ginger Goodroe. *There must be some mistake*, she thought. *That was definitely not the name on the email response.*

Ginger stuck out her hand, and April mechanically accepted it. "I'm so sorry, Ms. Saunders, that I tricked you, but I was afraid that you wouldn't see me if I used my real name."

April was still a bit dumbstruck. "Let's go back to the conference room," she said abruptly. Ginger followed her through the office.

When they were seated, April, who had been considering all the reasons Ginger might be here on their way to the conference room, asked, "So why are you here?"

"I want this job," Ginger replied simply.

"I thought you had a job at Oliver & Company."

"I do." Ginger hesitated. April could see the retiring personality that she had always witnessed while working at Nora's, but it quickly vanished as she continued. "Here's the thing. I don't want that job. I'm tired of being Donna's whipping boy, I mean, girl. I'll never get any further than I am now, and I'm better than that!" she announced with a flourish of her hand.

April smiled. "So you think you have what it takes to be a full editor?"

"I don't think; I know. I'm the one who's been doing Donna's work for the last three years. She's just been getting all the credit. Who do you think edited Mr. Blackridge's last novel? Not Donna, although she repeatedly takes credit for it." Ginger dropped her head. "I'm sorry for ranting. It's just that I'm so tired of the politics. I just want to be an editor."

"You're hired," April announced.

"What? Don't you want to see my credentials?"

"Why? I know you worked at Oliver & Company. Knowing Donna, I can wholeheartedly believe everything you've told me. Besides, your last two statements are what secured the position for you. I don't tolerate politics, and I am only interested in the quality of the work that you do."

Tearing up, Ginger said, "Oh, thank you, Ms. Saunders!"

"Thank you for being so honest. Wait here, and I'll get the necessary paperwork for you to fill out." As she left the conference room, she heard a quiet sob.

After Ginger filled out the paperwork, she waited for April to return. She jumped when John Blackridge spoke from the doorway. "I hear you edited my last novel at Oliver & Company."

Embarrassed and assuming he didn't believe her, she replied meekly, "Yes, I did." Almost apologetically, she added, "I know you think Donna did, but she didn't."

"I'm glad to hear it. You did a great job. I never liked Donna and finding out that she wasn't the one who did the editing is good news." He laughed. "You're going to have a lot of work to do around here. Are you ready for it?"

"Yes, sir!" she replied.

"You can call me John. We tend to be on a first-name basis around here — even April." Stepping in to shake her hand, he added, "See you in the morning."

"The morning?" she asked, slight panic in her voice.

"You don't really think Nora will let you work another day if she finds out you're going to work for April, do you?"

Mulling over his statement after he left, she knew he was right. Nora would probably throw her down the stairs after Donna verbally eviscerated her.

Chapter 22

Nearly three years later

"Are you sure you want to take me on?" April laughed, stepping back to get a better view of John's face.

"I don't think I have much choice," he replied, reaching out to pull her closer.

"Wait a minute! No one's forcing you." There was a defiant expression on her face.

"I don't have much choice because I can't imagine living without you around, bullying me."

"What!?" she snapped.

Laughing, John pulled her close, despite her protests. "I love you, you nitwit. Of course, I have no choice."

Melting into his arms, April fervently hoped that things would never change. The last few years had been wonderful. Center Stage had climbed to the top of the small press heap with no regrets. She and John had walked arm-in-arm to many awards functions. Tonight, three of their recent publications had been honored. She now had at least twenty authors of exceptional caliber, three editors, and two assistant editors. Ginger was her senior editor.

April couldn't help but smile when she thought about the gem she had snagged out from under Nora Oliver's nose without even trying. It was for the best. From what she had heard last month, Nora would be closing her doors soon.

****

Nora stood in the reception area and looked for the last time at the office that had been her life for forever. They had not yet taken down the letters spelling out Oliver & Company behind the reception desk. An indescribable urge to tear them off the wall passed through her. She quickly tried to quell the feeling and turned toward the elevator. Before she could stop herself, however, she was standing behind the reception desk, pulling the letters off the wall. *Let them sue me*, she thought as she stacked them on the desk. *It's not like they'll be able to rent the office to some company with the same name.* With a satisfied sigh, she pulled the last letter off the wall just as the elevator dinged.

Reaching her condo a few minutes later, she struggled to open the door without dropping "Oliver & Company." Setting the letters down on the bar counter, she looked around the living room. The wall across from her held framed awards she had accumulated over the years. She strode across the room and began taking them off the wall, one by one. Going to the utility closet, she pulled out a tape measure and a roll of double-sided tape. Grabbing the letters, she laid them out carefully on the floor along the wall. Measuring the length, she marked the beginning line and ending line. First, she placed the O. Next, she placed the y. Trusting her ability to eyeball the spacing, she placed the l and then the n, continuing until all that was left was the & and the space before it.

"Perfect!" she declared. Laying out the framed awards, she decided on a layout and proceeded to finish up her Wall of Memories. When she stepped back to admire her handiwork, she realized memories were all that was left of her life now.

Donald, her husband, was gone; Oliver & Company, her surrogate child, was gone. Her "family" was gone, too. Ginger had jumped ship early, but Nora knew it was best for her. She was young and needed to carve out a place of her own. Her betrayal by going to work for April had hurt though. Donna, appropriately named since she was certainly a prima donna, had not been kind when it came time to shut the doors. Sandra and Lindsey had cried. Nora had to admit the one she missed the most was Jean Wilson. Jean was eccentric, but you would never find a better editor.

On the last day of work, Jean had whispered in her ear as she hugged her, "Sometimes the past has to be ripped away from us before we're strong enough to move into something better. You will be okay, Nora, and so will I."

Nora had not really been able to relate to her words that day, but now she was wondering if she was right. Looking at her Wall of Memories, she suddenly felt an incredible lightness of spirit. Perhaps

Jean had been right. Although she had no idea where she was going from here, at least she was financially protected, thanks to Donald. Donald had known her so well. She had always invested all her monies into the company. When he died, his arrangements prevented her from withdrawing any additional monies from the trust he had left her. She was provided with an allowance that was more than adequate to live the life to which she was accustomed, but not enough to keep her company afloat. When he died, she had been angry that he did not trust her to manage her own affairs. Now, she was simply grateful.

Chapter 23

The wedding had been the stuff of fairy tales. The society pages were filled with photos of the bride and groom, many describing April as a goddess. She had allowed her golden hair to fall loose over her shoulders. Having chosen ivory, supposedly since she had been married before but really because it highlighted her hair, April fell in love with a trumpet gown. When she tried it on, it fit perfectly, hugging her body until mid-hip when it gradually widened until reaching the floor. It was strapless with a sweetheart neckline outlining a bodice of shirred tulle. Beaded lace forming small, four-petal flowers covered the entire gown. A cathedral veil, elegantly edged with lace and beads, swept from a perfectly exquisite tiara to the floor and beyond the sweep train of her dress. The tiara was a gift from Laney Whitcombe. Pearls and diamonds accentuated the romantic design of gold, blending beautifully with her gown.

Every time April thought back to their honeymoon, she couldn't help but smile. She had never expected to get married again, much less have a romantic honeymoon. The memory of that first night was still fresh in her mind. John had been so sweet, acting as if they hadn't been together for years already. He had arranged everything, right down to the last romantic detail. It had been so tempting to just stay there and pretend that the dog-eat-dog world didn't exist outside. Yet, she had to admit that the dog-eat-dog world was where she felt the most comfortable. She could never really have stayed in that fairy tale. She would eventually have chewed her way out if necessary. Still, it was nice to muse over it occasionally.

Sitting at her desk today was one of those days. Looking out the window, she wondered if their marriage would last or become the stuff of tabloids. Tonight would be the test, she thought. The phone buzzed, interrupting her pondering.

"Yes?"

"Hi, sweetie! Are you ready to close it down for the day?"

Looking around her desk to see if there were any loose ends, she replied, "It looks like this is as good a time as any."

"Meet you in the lobby," John said, hanging up.

A short time later, they were sitting in their living room, eating delivery pizza and drinking beer. "John, I have something to tell you," she said, dropping her pizza back onto the plate.

Her serious expression rattled John. He didn't know what to expect. "What is it, April?" he asked, dreading to hear her answer.

Not one to beat around the bush, she blurted out, "I'm pregnant."

"What?" John was dumbfounded. He was expecting terrible news. This was wonderful! "That's the best news I've ever had!"

Screwing up her mouth, she blew out her breath through her nose. "I don't know—"

"What do you mean, you don't know?" John never dreamed he would have children, but the moment the word pregnant slipped through her lips, his whole world had shifted on its axis.

"I don't know if I want to have it."

John thought he must be hearing things. This was not possible. How could she not want a child who was the creation of their love? He shook his head, thinking he must have drunk too much beer. "I'm sorry. I'm just not understanding what you're saying."

Quite unaffected, April repeated, "I don't know if I want to have it."

John could sit still no longer. He leaped to his feet and headed toward the bar, but just before reaching it, he whirled around and headed back to the sofa. He sat down, facing April. "How can you say that? I don't understand." Tears rolled down his face.

April, much to her surprise, was shaken by the passion flowing from her husband. Until this moment, it had seemed a decision like any other — do it or not. Now, she wasn't sure. She couldn't imagine herself pregnant. She just didn't have time for all that. Still, it was John's child, too. *Strange,* she thought, *I haven't actually thought of it as a child until now.*

"April!" John's plea stirred her from her thoughts. "You can't be serious. Tell me why you would even think about this."

Hesitating, she tried to explain, "I just don't have time, John. I have a company to run and lots of people depending on me, you included."

"That's not a problem. I can take care of our child. I'm a writer. I can write as well here as I can at the office, probably better." He reached for her hand. "Sweetheart, this is a blessing. I never thought I would have a child. Please don't take this away from me, from us."

For the first time in her life, April let someone else's needs take precedence over her own, with conditions of course. "If I do, you have to promise me that you will never let it interfere with the business."

Grinning from ear to ear, John promised.

Chapter 24

Nearly nine years later

"You just don't understand!" April shouted. "I have meetings with important clients this evening. I can't just cancel on them. If they think I'm not interested, they'll go somewhere else!"

"So what?" snapped John, his jaw clenching. "It's not like you need any more clients. You are now the biggest so-called small press in the country. What difference will these two clients make?"

"That's not the point!" April yelled, not caring if anyone in the office could hear.

"Then what is the point? That you don't care enough about your daughter to go out to dinner with us to celebrate her eighth birthday?" John's tone was harsh.

"Don't take that tone with me. Where would you be without Center Stage Press and me—"

"Oh, god! You're not going down that road again, are you? It's getting rather lame." John shook his head, a look of disgust on his face.

"It's reality, John—"

"No! Reality is that I would have been all right without you. I might have struggled a bit, but I am a good writer, and it has nothing to do with you. Reality is that without you, I would never have had a daughter. That is the one thing I could never wish to undo. For her, I put up with your ego and your self-absorption.

"Do you realize that you have not actually been 'available' for any of Hannah's birthdays? Oh, you may eventually arrive, after the party's over. Well, she's getting old enough now that she is going to start to notice, and it's going to affect her feelings toward you. Up 'til now, you've gotten away with it, but that will start to change."

April sniffed, "You are always so melodramatic! She's just a kid. As long as there's money for her toys and pretty clothes and trips to Disneyland, I doubt she'll notice. Then when she gets to be a teenager, she won't want either of us around."

John gazed at this woman with whom he had fallen in love so long ago. He realized now he had misjudged the extent of her drive. He never dreamed it would take priority over family, over the love between them. John had to admit that he did still love her, but he was finding it increasingly difficult to like her, especially when it came to her decisions about Hannah.

"Fine," he said, "but I am through making excuses to her for you. From now on, you'll have to suffer the consequences of your own actions." With that, he walked out of her office and slammed the door.

Thoughts of Hannah crept into his mind as he headed back to the condo, dissolving the anger. She was the most wonderful thing that had ever happened to him, including the success of his novels. It was sad April didn't even really know her little girl. In just a short time, barely longer than she had been alive, she would be heading out the door to live her own life. These were days you could never recover. *Didn't April know that? Did she even care?* he wondered.

Opening the door of the condo, he was nearly knocked off his feet as Hannah ran and grabbed him around his hips. "Oh, Daddy! Guess what Miss Laney gave me!"

John laughed. Laney had always adored Hannah, for which he was eternally grateful. Hannah thought of her like a grandmother. Nodding at the babysitter, he said, "I could never guess in a million years! What did she get you this time?"

"It's beautiful! I can be just like you, Daddy!" Confused, John looked around and spotted a small antique writing desk with a matching chair. On top was a laptop computer. Bookends held a dictionary and a thesaurus.

"It *is* beautiful! After school, you can do your homework on it, and on weekends, you can start your first novel. How does that sound?"

Hannah hugged him tightly. "It sounds wonderful," she sighed.

"Right now, you have to get ready for our birthday celebration." He walked to the coat closet and reached up on the top shelf. "Guess what I have for you to wear tonight?" Hannah squealed. His heart expanding in his chest, John watched as Hannah tore the paper off the package.

"Oh, Daddy! It's a grown-up dress!" Her eyes sparkled as she fingered the soft, silky material. "It's my favorite color, too! How did you know?"

"There's not much I don't know about you, sweetheart." He was so glad she liked it. "Well, don't just stand there. Go get dressed. Miss Laney will be here any minute."

****

John tucked Hannah in. She was tuckered after her birthday celebration. Laney, Devon, and several other of John's friends along with five of her school friends and their parents had closed the place down. No one mentioned April. They were all used to her absences. John took one last look before he shut the light off.

"Daddy," Hannah said quietly, "why doesn't Mommy like me?" John stopped dead. He could barely bring himself to turn around because he didn't know what he was going to say. Throwing his shoulders back, he turned to meet the greatest challenge he had faced in his life.

"Why do you think that, sweetie?" Hoping that her reply would be something other than what he had predicted earlier that day, he sat down on the edge of the bed. Her raven black hair was spread out on the pillow, and his own gray eyes were mirrored in her sweet face.

"The mommies of all my friends came to my party. Even Miss Laney and Uncle Devon. It was my birthday. Why didn't Mommy come?"

Well, he thought, it was happening sooner than he had expected, sooner than he had had time to plan for. He decided to take one gentle step at a time. "You know Mommy is a very busy woman. She has a great big company to run." He knew he was reneging on his promise to April to make her face the consequences of her actions, but it was too hard. For that to happen, he had to hurt his little girl.

"I know that Daddy, but it's not just my birthday party. She never goes anywhere with us. Does she not like you either?"

The question stunned John. As ridiculous as it might sound, he had been so focused on how she treated Hannah, it had never occurred to him that perhaps she no longer loved him. He had blamed her actions on her obsessive drive to succeed. He had never thought she might be deliberately avoiding him as well as Hannah.

"Daddy?" Hannah sat up in bed. The look on her daddy's face was scaring her. "Are you okay?"

Shaken out of the sudden numbness he had felt by her statement, John put his arms around her and held her tightly. "Yes, sweetie. I'm just fine. It's late. Let's talk about all this later. Okay?"

Hannah agreed and let him tuck her in again, but as he walked away, she wondered why he looked so sad.

The next day, John was determined to confront April. It wasn't fair to put Hannah through this. If April didn't want them in her life, he would take Hannah and leave. She couldn't fire him. Years earlier, he had been angry at first when he realized his contract, unlike Laney's and Devon's, would keep him tied to her for the rest of his life. Then he had chosen to see it as a romantic gesture — proof she wanted him with her forever. Now, however, the bubble had burst, and he realized he was simply her lifesaver, one bestselling author who could never leave Center Stage Press. There were always two sides to a coin, so it meant she was stuck with him, too. Whether she liked it or not, Center Stage Press would have to support him and Hannah for the rest of their lives.

Not wanting to give April any warning or take the chance of Hannah being in earshot, John headed for the office to talk. He didn't bother asking if April was free. He simply walked into her office without even knocking. She was on the phone.

"Hang up," he said.

April looked at him like he was insane and continued her conversation.

"Hang up," he said loudly, "or I will hang it up for you."

"Fine," she said, covering the receiver with her hand. "Charles, I have an emergency here in the office with one of the staff. Can I call you back shortly?

"Thanks. I'll get right back to you."

"Is that what I am to you," snapped John, "one of the staff?"

"During office hours, yes," she retorted.

Whatever reservations had existed before were washed away, and John had a clear path open in front of him. "I want a divorce, and I will be taking Hannah. You *will* pay child support for her. At least it will force you to face the fact that you have a daughter." April was speechless.

"Don't even think about trying to manipulate this situation to stay in control. You have no control over your daughter. You don't even have a relationship with her. Do you know what she asked me last night? She wanted to know why you didn't like her. I once again lied for you. I can't keep that up so I'm going to take you out of the equation." April simply stared at him. John wasn't used to this silent routine so he thought it best to finish up and leave. "You will hear from my lawyer in the next few days. Don't even think about contesting it. If you do, you will regret it." With that, he turned and walked out of her office.

John went straight to his lawyer's office. Terry Hall was in and glad to see John. After explaining the circumstances regarding April's relationship with Hannah and the custody arrangements, John said, "Also, Hannah and I will remain in the condo, which has been her home all her life. April will have to move elsewhere.

"I also want to draw up a separate agreement regarding the termination of her contractual hold on me and my works. Any books that were published by Center Stage Press will continue under the same royalties agreements as long as she does not allow them to go out of print. If she does, they automatically revert to me, and she will no longer receive royalties on those books.

"In addition, I want it stipulated that this business agreement in no way affects the child support she is expected to pay for Hannah's care."

"Is that all?" asked Terry. "Do you want them both served at the same time?"

John had to think for a moment. "What do you think?"

"Well, it's rather touchy. If you serve the divorce papers first, she may not feel obliged to agree to the contractual changes. If you serve the business papers first, we can add a cover letter stating that divorce papers are to follow, which will outline her future personal and financial relationship with her daughter and with you. It's not a direct threat, but it might give her pause. She may consider that it might get worse if she doesn't sign these first."

John didn't really think that her relationship with Hannah mattered that much to her, but it was probably wise to serve the business papers first. If he could free himself of her, he would only have to deal with her accountant, and he wouldn't have to make excuses to Hannah for her.

Chapter 25

John couldn't really say that life had been that different since the divorce was finalized over three years ago. Just like before, April had made no effort to spend time with Hannah. He had offered to let her have Hannah over Thanksgiving that first year, but April had refused, saying she was in the middle of important negotiations. The next year he had informed April she was going to spend time with her daughter over spring break whether she liked it or not, but this time Hannah refused to go. John gave up. Why force two people together who had no desire to be together? He had sat down with Hannah at the time, not knowing what to say. Even the writer in him came up with nothing.

"It's all right, Daddy," Hannah had said before he spoke. "I understand. Mommy doesn't want to be with me or you, and that's okay. I don't hate her, but I have to be honest with you. I don't really like it when she's around. She just makes everyone nervous and grouchy."

John couldn't help but laugh remembering her little speech. Quite a kid for ten years old. At the time, of course, he had told her that if she ever wanted to see her mother he would take her. She had merely nodded before heading into the kitchen for something to eat.

As he had suspected, April's pride wouldn't let him stay at Center Stage Press so she had let all his books with her press go out of print over the two years after the divorce was final. Her lawyer had recently sent him a letter, informing him that publishing rights for his titles had reverted to him. He wasn't rushing to republish any of them. He was still doing quite well financially from his books pre-April. Oliver & Company had indeed shut their doors, but Nora had sold her remaining assets to another press, which had been faithfully paying royalties to him.

He was steadily writing. As a matter of fact, he had finished three manuscripts. Each was better than the last in his opinion, but he had not approached anyone about publishing them. The twelve years he had spent with April had made him skittish about stepping back into the publishing industry. He had a meeting today with a web designer. Perhaps an interactive web site could generate some interest in his available books. He had seen some other big name writers doing it, and it seemed to be paying off for them. Besides, if he did move ahead with his recovered books and publish his new manuscripts, he could use the web site to promote all of his books, not just the ones with a particular publisher.

The meeting did not go as well as he had hoped. The web designer was less of a designer and more of an assembly line person—*tell me what to put together, and I'll assemble it for you.* John wanted someone creative, who could tell *him* what he needed—not the other way around. It had only taken fifteen minutes for him to send the man packing.

Nursing his second drink, John looked up just in time to see Nora Oliver emerge from the restroom and head for a table. *Oh, my god! What else can go wrong tonight?* He ducked his head, moving his food around with a fork until he was sure she had had time to get to her table. Taking a few more bites and downing the rest of his drink in a single gulp, John glanced at his phone, which had started vibrating on the table. Incoming Call. Nora Oliver.

Oh, shit! She saw me, which means I have to take this call. His hand hovered over the phone, hoping it would stop vibrating. Realizing he was trapped, he picked it up. "Hello?" he said.

"Why don't you join me for dessert?" Nora asked.

John hesitated, not knowing whether to admit he knew she was in the restaurant or not. "Come on, John. I won't bite. I'm at a table near the front window."

"Sure, let me tell my waiter, and I'll be glad to join you."

"Good." Nora hung up.

Waiting for his waiter to look in his direction, John realized that he was rather glad she had called. He had always hated the way their relationship had ended. He didn't think he would have done anything differently, but still …

After ordering another drink and telling his waiter where he would be, John headed toward the front room of the restaurant. God, he hoped that her life was not in a shambles. Ashamed to admit it to himself, he had not kept up with her after Oliver & Company closed. Just as the dread was starting to creep in, he spotted her. She waved him over. *She looks happy and well*, he thought.

"Sit down, John. It's been a really long time!" She waved her hand in the direction of the chair across from her.

"You're looking great, Nora!"

"Relax, John," Nora admonished. "I survived April Saunders *and* you! Actually I have never been happier in my life, except perhaps when Donald was alive."

Relieved that she seemed in such good spirits, John was still grateful when the waiter arrived with his drink. "What are you doing these days?"

"A better question is what are you doing these days? I heard that you and April divorced. When was it — about three years ago?" John nodded. "I've also heard that you are raising your daughter Hannah."

"My, you have quite a pipeline of information," John replied nervously. He wasn't sure where this was heading, but it was starting to feel like an inquisition.

" I also know that you regained publishing rights for your Center Stage novels."

"You always did have your ear to the ground. Guess some things never change." He picked up the dessert menu and pretended to browse.

"I've already ordered our dessert. My treat." She reached out and took the menu from his hand and laid it on the table. "I have something I want to ask you, John."

"Okay" was all he could manage. The primitive instinct of fight or flight was stirring, and he was leaning toward flight. However, he settled back in his chair, attempting to appear relaxed, making sure his drink was within reach.

"John, I know we have a checkered past, but it seems that the facilitator responsible for taking us down divergent paths is no longer an influence on either of our lives. Am I right?"

John reluctantly agreed. Although he believed April's behavior abhorrent, he had never quite shaken that spark that had always been there. If it hadn't been for Hannah, he might still be her willing puppet.

Watching his face, Nora couldn't stop her next question before it leaped from her mouth. "You're not still in love with her, are you?"

Shocked by the question, John looked across the table at her for a moment before shaking his head. "No. I was just thinking of what might have been, but," he laughed, "if you recall, I don't write fantasy."

Nora guffawed. "No, you don't, thank God!"

The waiter arrived with their desserts and a carafe of coffee. "Your special blend, ma'am."

"Oh, don't tell me — it's not Robusta?"

"What else?" she shrugged. "So, what *are* you doing these days, John?"

"Writing, of course. Taking care of Hannah. She's heading toward her twelfth birthday in a few months. Ah, Nora, you can't imagine how wonderful it is to have such a gift come into your life," he sighed. Without even thinking about it, he reached into his inside jacket pocket and pulled out his wallet. Passing the picture across the table, he smiled.

"She's the spitting image of you!" Nora said, but she was thinking how fortunate it was that she wasn't a reminder of April.

Handing the picture back to John, Nora didn't let him off the hook. "What are you doing with your writing?" John tensed. "I'd like to see some of it."

"Why? I thought you were out of the business."

"Well, Oliver & Company is out of business for sure; however, I am not out of the business. Before I tell you what I'm doing, answer my question. Would you be willing to let me look at your manuscripts if you thought I could help you?"

He hesitated, feeling somewhat like he had taken a step back in time. Then he realized that meeting Nora like this might just be the synchronicity he needed to get his career back on track. "Yes. Yes, I would," he replied sincerely. "Now, it's your turn. What are you doing these days?"

Nora smiled. "Well, after Oliver & Company closed, I wasn't sure what to do. After a couple of years, my friend Abby Dickson invited me to visit her in New York. I wound up renting an apartment there for a while. I had a great time, getting to reacquaint myself with old friends in the business and making new ones. One morning I received a call from David Williams, a man I met at a cocktail party. He asked if I was in love with retirement or would I be up to the challenge of being an acquisitions editor for one of the Big Six. It took me about two seconds to answer him, and the rest is history. I've been with them almost ten years now."

John was flabbergasted. He had never heard anything about Nora's career shift. Of course, he hadn't actually asked anyone.

"Don't look so surprised," Nora remarked. "I'm quite good at it."

"I'm sure you are. It's just that no one has ever mentioned it. If April knows, she sure hasn't mentioned it — not that we talk anymore."

"I don't publicize it. It actually makes it easier for me to get the straight story on authors and books if they don't realize who I am."

"I can see that."

"Bottom line, John. Will you let me see your manuscripts?"

"Where do you want me to send them?" he asked without hesitation.

"Here's my card," she said, reaching across the table. "I have an office here and in New York since I have apartments in both places. Send it to my Chicago office. I'll be here for a couple more weeks."

John fingered the card. "Can I ask you something?" Nora nodded. "Is this about revenge or is it about me as a writer?" He expected her to scream at him, but she just chuckled.

"I have no reason to seek revenge on you, John. You did what any business person should do — take care of their business — regardless of my reaction at the time. You were one of my best writers, if not the best. I'm sure you haven't lost your touch. Having you on board will benefit me, and I'm sure it will help your career get back on track. As far as April is concerned, I think life will eventually have its way with her. I see no reason to interfere."

"Thank you," he responded sincerely. Looking at his watch, he stood. "I have to get home to Hannah. It's been a pleasure to see you again, Nora, and I will send the manuscripts in the morning." He reached out to shake her hand, hoping this was his chance to be a sought-after writer again.

Chapter 26

April was in her office reading the latest news on the Publishers Weekly web site when a headline nearly caused her to spit her coffee all over her keyboard.

John Blackridge Signs With Major Publishing House
Dropping Center Stage Press Wise Move

"What the hell? He didn't drop me. I dropped him!" she screamed. Everyone in the bullpen scattered, not wanting to be the victim of her obvious wrath. Her assistant, however, had nowhere to go.

"Julie, get in here!" April bellowed, not bothering with the intercom. Julie stepped into her office, remaining as near to the door as possible.

"Get me the person in charge at Publishers Weekly on the phone. He and I are going toe-to-toe! I will not sit still while he slanders my company!"

Flinching, Julie quickly retreated.

In a few minutes, April's phone buzzed to let her know her call was ready. Grabbing the receiver, she demanded, "Am I speaking to the person in charge of the new articles on your web site?"

"It depends on the nature of your inquiry, ma'am," a young woman's voice replied.

"I want to talk to whoever approved the online article about John Blackridge."

"I'm sorry, but the Senior Web Editor left on vacation this morning. Perhaps I can help you?"

Fuming, April snapped, "I doubt it. I want to know who chose to slander my company, Center Stage Press, with that headline."

"Ah," the young woman said. "I'm afraid that there is no slander involved, ma'am. It was simply a statement of fact. Center Stage Press has obviously done nothing to promote Mr. Blackridge's career in recent years. Therefore, moving up the ladder to one of the Big Six would definitely qualify as a wise move."

Flustered by the woman's cool explanation, April was silent for a moment too long.

"Thank you for calling, Ms. Saunders." The phone buzzed in April's ear. She was incensed by the fact that the woman knew her name. Of course, she had identified herself as the owner of Center Stage, but somehow it had felt like the woman was mocking her.

Slamming the receiver down, April went back to PW Online to read the actual article. As much as she would like to be, she couldn't be upset that John had gotten back into the game. He was too good a writer to give it up, and, besides, he hadn't said anything derogatory about her or Center Stage. That was entirely the fault of some PW staff member.

****

The table looked like a Party City clearance sale. There were “Happy 12th Birthday” balloons tied to the centerpiece alongside balloons declaring "Congratulations.” Sparkling confetti littered the table and the floor around their table. On one side of the centerpiece sat a cake with white icing and pink swirls along the sides. On top was a miniature typewriter. Underneath, written in blue letters, it read "Happy Birthday, Hannah!" On the other side of the centerpiece was a second, but smaller cake in the shape of a book. The sides were decorated to look like the pages and spine of a book. On the top, it read "A New Beginning" with John Blackridge written underneath.

John, Hannah, Laney, and Devon were having a dual celebration for Hannah's twelfth birthday and John's breakthrough. The announcement had appeared in Publishers Weekly that morning, so Laney believed a joint celebration was in order. She knew Hannah wouldn't mind sharing the spotlight with her dad.

"Oh, Miss Laney, I just love the little typewriter! I'm going to keep it on my desk as an inspiration."

Laney laughed. "Girl, if that's all it takes, I'm going straight away tomorrow and get me one!"

"You don't need inspiration. It just flows out of you. I've read every one of your books!" Hannah declared.

"You have?" Strange, but Laney had never thought about Hannah reading her books.

"Absolutely! You and Dad, and Devon of course, are my silent mentors."

"We are?" they all said simultaneously.

With a mischievous smile, Hannah remarked, "You did notice that I said *silent* mentors." They all laughed, knowing that Hannah would never reject suggestions from any of them related to writing. She was well into her first novel and very excited about it even though she hadn't offered to let anyone read it yet.

Laney would be mortified if anyone found out, but she had sneaked a peek one afternoon while Hannah was in school. She had been waiting on John to finish getting dressed for a happy hour cocktail party and had wandered over to Hannah's desk. She slid her hand across the desk, remembering when she had bought this for her. Without thinking, she opened the side drawer, and there it was, a temptation that was stronger than she. Quickly scanning the first chapter, she realized that Hannah had inherited her father's writing genes. Her descriptions and ability to draw the reader in were incredible for one so young. She had wanted to read more but had heard John turn off the shower, and she didn't want to get caught.

"Well, since I did buy you your writing desk and your new inspirational charm, I would like to ask you how your novel is coming." John cleared his throat, a little uncomfortable with Laney putting Hannah on the spot, but he needn't have worried.

Hannah quickly replied, "It's wonderful! I have never felt so alive as when I'm telling this story. Now I understand why all of you are so dedicated to your writing. I think mine might even be a bestseller!"

Devon spewed his drink, and Laney and John burst out laughing.

"What? Don't you think I could write a bestseller?" Hannah asked, a little hurt by their reactions.

"Honey," her dad said, "it's not that. We all just wish we had had your attitude when we started out, much less at twelve years old." Wiping tears from her eyes, Laney agreed. Devon nodded, busy wiping up his mess.

Raising her glass, Laney said, "A toast to Hannah, a beginning writer, and to John, who is beginning again.

"Hear! Hear!" shouted John as they all clinked glasses.

Chapter 27

Laney was sitting in her office at Center Stage Press. She had endured yet another one of April's tirades earlier in the afternoon. They were getting worse. Last week she had confided in John she was starting to question April's sanity. Seeing how upset she was, he reluctantly told her about the cyclothymia diagnosis when April was young and that it was a mild version of bipolar disorder.

"Mild, my ass!" Laney had sworn. "She's just about neutered everyone on the staff. I'm not sure how long we'll be able to keep the ones who aren't under contract."

John had to admit to Laney he was shocked. He couldn't imagine April letting herself lose control enough to endanger her business, despite the disorder. The thought of April not being in control of herself and everyone around her was difficult for him to get his head around. Still, he hadn't been around her in several years, and Laney assured him she was seriously out of control.

Tonight the office was quiet. Laney had sat in the dark like a teenager trying to avoid her parents until she heard April locking the front door. It was hard to do anything with April around because she never knocked. If your door was shut, she considered it an invitation to interrupt. Laney wanted to study the office copy of her contract in peace and see if there was a way out. Her lawyer had her copy, and she didn't want to wait until tomorrow. If she went home tonight without looking at it, she would fret all night.

As soon as she heard the elevator bell ding, she crept out into the bullpen, ran her hand around under the bookkeeper's middle desk drawer until she felt the key to the file cabinet with the legal files in it.

Laney hadn't looked at her contract in years. It was partly laziness on her part. She had gotten used to Chicago, and she wasn't getting any younger. She just never thought she would have to consider a life change again. Perhaps John's reentry into the publishing game in such a big way had made her a bit envious, but she also knew it had made it all the more difficult to put up with April's fits.

Digging her contract out of the file cabinet, she sat down at the bookkeeper's desk and began to read. After about three pages, she cried out, "Oh, my god!" Marking her place with her finger, she flipped to the back page and began calculating in her head. "Oh, my god! I'm free!" She realized that it had been fifteen years and ten months since she had signed the contract with Center Stage Press. She stared at a magical line in front of her: *After the fifteen year period, termination of the contract may be made by either party without explanation.*

First thing in the morning, she was going to see her attorney.

****

Sitting at Starbucks, Laney nursed her mocha latte while John sipped his espresso, waiting for her to speak. Finally, he pleaded, "Come on, Laney. You're freaking me out here. Say something!"

Smiling, which John took as a good sign, she said, "Well, I've been trying to figure out how I feel."

"About *what*?"

"About what I've just done."

"Are you trying to torture me? If you don't spit it out right now, I'm taking my espresso to another table," John declared.

Laughing, Laney replied, "Don't get your knickers in a wad." Taking a deep breath, she continued. "I just terminated my contract with Center Stage Press."

"You did what!" John was stunned.

"Why? Are you thinking it was a wrong move? Look, I was sick to death of her tirades. Writing is supposed to be fun. Oh, I know there's a business side to it, but it doesn't have to be akin to having your teeth pulled without anesthesia."

John reached across the table to his dearest friend and grasped her hand. "No, I don't think it was a bad idea. I was just shocked after all this time."

"Yeah, well, seeing you escape a few years back wasn't too discouraging, at least not until April finally went off her nut, but then you hooked up with Nora. That's when I started wondering if there actually were greener pastures out there, even for someone who is as far over the hill as I am."

John chuckled, unable to view his friend that way. "I only hope I'm as alert, astute, and in step with my target audience as you when I'm your age."

"You don't have to make it sound like I'm an anthropological anomaly," she whined. John ignored her. He knew when she was baiting him.

"So what's next for you?"

"Don't know," she said, looking around the room. "Maybe I'll be discovered by an acquisitions editor while I'm drinking my mocha latte." She chuckled, but there was a touch of desperation in her voice.

Holding up his cup, John said, "Here's to a bright and fun-filled future!"

With forced frivolity, Laney clinked her cup to his, thinking of last month when they had toasted his new beginning. She only hoped she hadn't made a mistake.

Chapter 28

At The Crossroads Restaurant

Grace watched as April twitched in her chair, a frown creasing her brow. Tossing her hand slightly in the air, Grace sat quietly as April again emerged from her trance.

"Enough!" she shouted. "I don't want to see the rest."

"Why, my dear? You've been through your part of this before. You know what's ultimately going to happen. Why are you so upset?" Grace was trying to draw April into a place of self-observation where she could truly face herself. It was the only way.

"I don't want to see the rest! Isn't that enough?" she demanded as she started to rise from her chair. Grace again waved her hand, and April discovered that she could not get up.

"What is this? You can't keep me here," April snapped, fear starting to set in.

"Actually, dear, I have permission to do whatever it takes." Grace smiled sweetly at April.

"Whatever it takes for what?" April retorted as she tried in vain to force the chair away from the table. Finally, she quit struggling and sat limply in the chair.

"That's much better, dear. This is for your own good. You cannot go through life stepping on people without there being a price to pay. Watching what led you to your present state is surely minor compared to the price you've already paid."

April didn't respond. As Grace raised her hand into the air, April moaned, powerless to stop what was to come.

Chapter 29

After finding out that Laney had left Center Stage, John was both excited and worried for her. Although she had been on the bestseller list for the last decade and a half with her mysteries after years of the same with her romance novels, John wasn't sure how hard it would be for her at her age to be considered a valued asset. How many more years would she want to write?

Picking up the phone, he dialed Nora's cell.

"Hi, John! I was planning to call you this evening."

"Really? What about?" He couldn't help but tense up. Being back in the game was still nerve-wracking for him.

"I'm going to be in Chicago tomorrow, and I thought we might have dinner."

"Is there a problem?" His gut clenched.

"No, of course not. I just couldn't think of anyone with whom I'd rather have dinner," she laughed.

Breathing a sigh of relief, he said, "Well, as it so happens, I wanted to talk with you about something."

"Good news? Bad news?"

"I hope it turns out to be good news." John was already feeling awkward about the whole idea. He had hoped to talk to her in person about it.

"Well, go ahead and spit it out. I'm not good at waiting."

After a short pause, John asked, "Would you be interested in interviewing a possible client?"

"Depends. Are they new or do they have experience?"

"Oh, she has lots of experiences. Tons of it."

"Quit beating around the bush, John. Just tell me who it is."

"Laney Whitcombe." John held his breath.

"*The* Laney Whitcombe?" John couldn't help but smile as he

remembered April saying the same thing so many years ago. "The Center Stage Laney Whitcombe?" Nora asked.

"Yes, that Laney Whitcombe. I'm sure you know she has been just as big a success as a mystery writer as she was writing romance novels."

Nora laughed. "Do you think I've been hiding in a hole somewhere, John?"

Embarrassed by his clumsy comment, John said, "No, it's just that she left Center Stage Press recently."

"Why?" Nora inquired.

"Can I be honest with you and it stay confidential?"

"You know me well enough that you shouldn't need to ask that question."

"You're right, but it's kind of touchy." Clearing his throat, he said, "Laney was fed up with April's tirades, which seem to be getting worse. She said writing was no longer fun."

"How did she get out of her contract? I heard through the grapevine that you had to practically threaten April to get out of yours."

John wondered what else the grapevine had said. "Well, I found out after the fact that my contract and those Laney and Devon signed were not identical. For some strange reason, she gave them an out. Of course, she owned them for fifteen years, but after that, they could terminate the contract themselves."

"She probably figured they would have run their course by that time, and it would be good riddance."

"Whatever her reason, Laney took the time to study her contract after all these years and discovered what she calls that magic sentence that set her free."

Nora laughed. John waited. Finally, Nora broke the suspense. "I would be out of my friggin' mind to turn down the chance to acquire Laney Whitcombe."

John was surprised to feel a tear track its way down his cheek.

"Have you spoken to her about this?" Nora asked.

"No. I didn't want to get her hopes up and then squash them." John could hear Nora breathing but decided to let her make the next move.

"You know what, John? I want to apologize to you for screaming at you all those years ago. You've paid a hefty price *but* gained as much from your decision back then, and I can't say that I regret the outcome for me either. What I'm doing now is so much more fun, and the responsibilities are much easier to carry. Maybe it was our crossroads, and we're both better off because of it."

Already feeling vulnerable, John heard a quiet sob escape his throat. "Thank you, Nora. I've always felt bad about all that, but I agree with you. I could never regret Hannah, but I was really glad to hear that you were okay."

"Enough of this mushy stuff. I'll call you when I get into Chicago, and we'll set a place to meet for dinner. In the meantime, you talk to Laney. If she's game, bring her with you."

****

Although he was sixteen years older, Devon hadn't really changed that much. He was still just as temperamental as he was when John first met him. He watched as Devon stirred his drink with such fervor that John scooted his chair away from the table a bit to avoid the potential spray. He had learned a long time ago to just wait Devon out. He would eventually come to grips with what he wanted to say.

Dropping the stir stick onto the napkin, Devon covered his mouth with a fist while he cleared his throat. "It's like this, John. April has been good to me, more or less, but now that you and Laney are both gone, things are different. I feel like I'm a reminder of what was—" He raised his hand to stave off John's remark. "Oh, I know that seems silly, but I swear she looks at me funny sometimes, and this weird shiver passes through me."

Laughter burst out of John, despite his effort to be serious. "I know she's scary sometimes, but I don't think she has demon powers."

"You go ahead and laugh, but you're not the only one left in the arena for an angry gladiator to slaughter!'

"What? You writing stories about ancient Rome now?" John was struggling to keep from guffawing.

"Give me a break. You know what I mean. She's a scary woman. I've managed to stay out of her way for the last fifteen years, but since Laney left, it's almost impossible."

"So you admit that you were hiding behind our skirts, so to speak, all these years?" Thoroughly enjoying this discourse, John continued to rib Devon. "Wait until I tell Laney!"

"Don't you dare tell Laney!"

Laney had slipped in without Devon noticing and was standing behind his chair. "Tell me what, Devon?" Startled, Devon jumped, throwing liquid everywhere. "Why is it you can never keep liquid in your mouth or your glass?"

Devon shrugged, his angst dissipating somewhat. Laney and John were at once his best friends and the most aggravating influences on his life. "You two have it made. You got out, and now you're in the big leagues."

Laney glanced at John. "Doesn't this sound a lot like that conversation we had sixteen years ago when Devon was sure he was going to get the short end of the stick when we first signed on with Center Stage?"

Rubbing his chin, John answered, "You're right! I remember that conversation. I also remember that we told him you and I would never leave him out in the cold, that we were all in this together. Isn't that right?" Laney nodded.

Devon piped up, "That was different. We're on different teams and not even playing in the same ball park now."

"Would you like to play for a different team and change ball parks?" John asked, carrying on with the analogy.

"What do you mean?"

"A simple question. I think you're astute enough to understand what I'm saying."

Looking from Laney to John, Devon's eyes lit up. "Do you mean it? Is it even possible?"

John picked up his phone and punched in a number. "I think he's ready to talk with you." Placing the phone on the table, John told Devon, "This is a crossroads for you. What you decide is up to you, but I would suggest that you seriously consider your options and choose wisely."

Devon looked up to see Nora Oliver standing beside his chair. "I understand we have something to discuss," she said.

When Devon looked across the table at his two best friends, he didn't know what to say. They smiled at him, and he fought to keep the tears from escaping.

Chapter 30

When John left Center Stage, April thought, it hadn't been so bad. People knew they had gotten a divorce and just assumed they didn't want to work together anymore. At first everything went on as usual. Then within a year-and-a-half time span, she'd had to replace two office employees, her bookkeeper and the receptionist. Still, there was always a certain amount of attrition in a workplace, right?

Then three years after John divorced her, Laney terminated her contract. After Laney left, those writers who could hightailed it out the door within short order. Just a minor bump in the road, she'd convinced herself. Then, within the year, Devon left. After her golden circle was gone, all hell broke loose. The first to resign was her long-time Senior Editor, Ginger Goodroe. Soon after, April realized she might have made a mistake with the writers she had brought onboard after her so-called "golden circle." She had allowed them to have short term contracts, 2-3 book deals. Most had stayed with her through the years, signing new contracts along the way. They were all good producers, but none could match the sales performances of her golden circle.

Today, she only had three authors who were still under contract, and they weren't producing enough to keep her afloat. Sure, she still had monies coming in, but if you didn't keep producing, you died, and April knew she was on her last breath. There was a time when authors called her to set up appointments. Now she couldn't even get a callback.

To make things even worse, the landlord had served her with an eviction notice two weeks ago because she couldn't afford the new lease terms. It seemed nothing was going right for her. Sitting on one of the desks the auction house movers hadn't carried out yet, she wondered once again how John, Laney, and Devon had all managed to sign on with the same publisher. She assumed John had managed to get them signed, but it wasn't like him to be vengeful so Laney and Devon must have pressured him.

Oh well, she thought, *that's history. I can survive. I still have my condo, and my three writers work out of their homes for the most part.*

When we need to meet, they can come to the condo. I can rebuild Center Stage. I'll just need to be careful about how I structure contracts from now on.

At that moment, a man dressed in a rack suit stepped inside the door. "April Saunders?"

"Yes, and who are you?" she asked, not bothering to stand.

Holding out three envelopes, he said, "You've been served." April made no move to take them. Without offering any reaction, he simply laid them on the desk before turning on his heel and leaving.

Stunned, April slid off the desk, leaving the envelopes where they laid. She walked across the office to the window looking out on the water. A sense of dread was pushing down on every cell in her body. A feeling of being cut loose from a tether overwhelmed her. It was at once freeing and terrifying. *How could this be happening to her again?*

"Hey, lady! I'm puttin' your mail on the floor. We need to move this desk out of here."

Waving her hand absently, April replied, "Whatever."

****

Word spread quickly that Center Stage Press had shut its doors. There was even a picture in the paper showing April leaving the building for the last time. Nora wasn't sure how she felt about it. She had every reason to hate April. She had hurt a lot of people. Still, things seemed to have worked out for most everybody in the long run. This morning she heard that April's last three authors had served her with papers demanding release from their contracts due to her current inability to fulfill her part of the contracts. It was doubtful April could fight and win when she couldn't even keep her doors open.

Nora couldn't help but feel that revenge, albeit unintended, did have a sweet edge to it. She had wound up acquiring April's three major producers without actively poaching them. She didn't think she could have lived with herself if she had set out to put April out of business. From what she had gathered from the scuttlebutt, April had done a good job of that herself. Why she wouldn't take meds to level out her moods was something Nora couldn't understand. Truth was that her escalating mood swings had done more damage, it seemed, than anything else — even her highly-inflated ego.

****

April experienced déjà vu as the last of her furniture was carried out of her condo to a moving van. A year earlier she had watched her office being cleaned out. The difference was she had still had dreams that day. Now, she had none.

She had been the target of entertainment shows and gossip magazines continuously over the last year. It seemed like there was no shortage of people to interview who were willing to trash her. One reporter even tried to interview Jeffrey Taber. *When reporters were willing to dig twenty years into your past,* she thought, *they're like starving hyenas stumbling upon fresh prey. Nothing can stop them.* She supposed it was a blessing that Jeffrey refused to discuss her with the press. Still, they had managed to dig up some scuttlebutt from long-term employees of his. She was surprised that Brandon Foster hadn't jumped at the chance to trash her. She supposed everything had something that could qualify as a silver-lining.

Thank God she had made sure that not all her money was tied up in the business and that she wasn't in trouble with the IRS. She wasn't broke, but she would be if she stayed in Chicago any longer. As difficult as it was for her, she was swallowing her pride and moving back to the small town in Mississippi where she was raised. She could have moved someplace where no one knew her, but the familiarity of it seemed to be a comfort, and she hadn't felt comfortable in quite a while. She also knew she could survive there financially for a long time. No one in her family was left, and it was unlikely anyone would remember her. An extra bonus was that she had taken the time to check the housing market and discovered that in such a depressed market, she could even afford to buy a house.

Maybe I'll write a book, she thought as she watched the movers wiggle the last piece of furniture out the front door. After all, she hadn't lost her touch when it came to creating storylines, and she was sure she could do a better job than most of the writers who had worked for her. However, like a lot of her ideas these days, this one floated out of her head as quickly as it had entered.

After locking the door, April walked to the elevator where she caught a glimpse of herself in the mirror hanging there and gasped. All her clothes were designed to hang loosely because she liked the freedom of it, but she hadn't realized how much weight she had lost in the last year. In her recent depressed state, she had rarely taken the time to look at herself, other than her face. *Oh well,* she thought dismissively as she stepped into the open elevator. Downstairs she gave her luggage to the doorman who helped the cabbie put them in the trunk.

Riding to the airport, she felt a twinge as they passed the building where John and Hannah lived. She had tried to call Hannah several times in the last month. For some reason she had just wanted to talk to her. Could it have been six years since she had seen her? Yes, she realized, it had been when the divorce was finalized. She had seen Hannah waiting at the car for John when they were leaving the courthouse. She was sure Hannah had seen her but had deliberately ignored her. Taking it to heart, April had never tried to contact her until recently. Apparently John had caller ID because no one ever answered the phone. She had only left a message twice.

Hannah was a teenager now, and April knew that if she had inherited any of her traits, it was likely she had a mind of her own. She really couldn't blame Hannah if she hated her. Still, she knew if she had it to do all over again, it probably wouldn't be any different. Her company had been her lifeblood, her reason for getting up in the morning.

A week after arriving in her home town, April found a house just outside of town in a small housing development that adjoined a farm on three sides and the highway on the other. With only about forty houses in the development, it wasn't likely that neighbors would be a problem. She wasn't sure she was ready for the demands of a social life.

At first April distracted herself by setting up her furniture and buying a few things for the house. That lasted about three weeks before she was bored to death. Then she tried reading, but it only reminded her of what she had lost. Within a short time, she was spending more time in a depressed state than a manic one, which was quite the reversal for her.

One morning she woke up feeling optimistic. It was so foreign these days she wasn't sure what it was at first. After a few minutes, she felt its familiar warmth flowing through her. She felt invincible again. Jumping out of bed, she showered and dressed quickly. *It's time for things to turn around for me,* she thought. *I've been down before, but it never stopped me, and it won't this time!*

Heading into town, April drove through the commercial areas to get a feel for what was happening in this town. Few national chains had managed to get a toehold with the exception of McDonald's. When she saw the town library, she parked and went in. Unlike when she was a child, there were very few books on the shelves, and their reference section was abysmal. Smiling, April headed out to find a bookstore. There only appeared to be one in town. The sign read "Books & More." April had no idea what the "more" was, but she intended to find out.

Pushing the door open, she was met with the sound of a tinkling bell. *How quaint,* she thought sarcastically. *This should be a snap.* Her old self was front and center.

"If you need anything, just let me know," a middle-aged woman with shoulder-length brown hair called out from the back of the store. Dressed in a silk blouse and a pair of skinny jeans tucked inside a pair of knee-high, black boots, she was quite attractive. Staring at the woman, April was briefly reminded of how much weight she had lost, and how much she needed her own hair styled, but she quickly pushed those thoughts aside. *You have to stay in control*, she reminded herself.

By the time she had looked around the store for a while, a plan was already forming in her mind. She could tell where the weak spots were and what could be done to improve the displays. She hadn't spent all those years in the publishing business without learning about the point of sale to the public.

Walking to the back of the store, April cleared her throat to get the woman's attention. Stepping down off a ladder, the woman smiled. "May I help you find something?"

"Oh, no. I've found everything I need," replied April.

The woman looked at her quizzically because April had nothing in her hands. "I'm sorry. I'm a bit confused."

"Are you the owner?"

Wary, she replied, "Yes, I am. How can I help you?"

"I'd like to purchase your store."

Stunned, the woman looked at April for a moment before sticking out her hand. "My name is Andy—short for Andrea—Greene and you are?"

Shaking Andy's hand, April replied, "My name is April Saunders, and I want to buy your bookstore."

"What if I don't want to sell?" Andy asked.

"Oh, I think you will once you've heard my offer." April's ego was at full throttle.

Shaking her head at such arrogance, Andy decided she didn't have time to fool around with this woman. "I'm sorry. I don't know who you are or who you think I am, but I am not interested in selling this store. It is my life."

"Humph. All I can say is that your life needs a major makeover."

"Excuse me?!" Andy's ire was rising to the surface, and she no longer cared whether this woman was a potential customer or not.

"I think you heard me. This store is sorely lacking. Your purchasing decisions are not in line with the public's buying habits. Your displays do little to encourage anyone to buy those books, not to mention that you're not promoting the newest bestsellers." April was gaining confidence with every utterance, certain this woman was no match for her.

"Lady, I don't care what you think about this store. It serves my community, and I do quite well, despite your assessment."

"Depends on what you mean by *quite well*," retorted April.

Steam practically coming from her ears, Andy demanded, "Who the hell do you think you are?"

"I am April Saunders. I was the owner of Center Stage Press, the largest press in the country outside of the Big Six until I retired about a year and a half ago," she announced proudly.

Andy burst out laughing and was unable to speak coherently for a few minutes. "That explains a lot," she finally said.

"What do you mean?" April was incensed at this woman's reaction.

"What? You think just because I live in a small Mississippi town and own a measly 4000 square foot bookstore that I don't read the newspapers or listen to TV?" April frowned. "Retired, my ass. I know all about you. You're that nut job who walked all over everyone to get where you did, and then got her comeuppance when everyone jumped ship.

"I wouldn't sell you my store if I was starving to death — oh, not because of what you did before, but because of how you just treated me. Who do you think you are? You're just a small town Mississippi girl who thought she could move to the big city and be somebody. Well, let me clue you in. If you were an ass before you left here, moving was not the answer. Maybe you need to stop trying to manipulate other people to your will and examine why your choices never seem to work out so well for you.

"Now, get out of my store and never come back."

April, speechless for one of the few times in her life, turned and walked out. She returned to her house and crawled into bed, clothes and all. Every day after that was pretty much the same. She kept waiting for the manic phase to present itself again, but it didn't. She just kept sinking deeper and deeper into self-pity until she couldn't get out of bed at all.

Chapter 31

At The Crossroads Restaurant

Grace waited for April to wake up on her own. She suspected that she was resisting stepping back into reality so she let her be. She signaled to Henry, the waiter, to bring them fresh tea and a pastry.

April kept her eyes closed. She felt like her life force had been drained from her. Reliving her own life was an emotional roller coaster, the highs unerringly followed by devastating lows, but seeing other people's lives as well was too much. Still, everyone else's lives had turned out okay except for hers. Why not her?

"Feeling a little sorry for yourself, dearie?" Grace asked. April opened her eyes. "Here, have a drink of tea and a bite of pastry. It will fortify you." She slid the pastry dish toward her.

Submissively, April reached out for a pastry, but she didn't take a bite. She just laid it on the plate in front of her. Her mouth was too dry for her to speak, much less eat pastry. Taking a big gulp of iced tea, she glared at Grace. "Are you satisfied?"

Shaking her head slightly, Grace responded, "And what would I be satisfied about?" Grace could feel the resistance in April.

"You got to watch me suffer through my whole miserable life again, not to mention seeing how well everyone else is doing."

"Does that bother you?"

"What?"

"Seeing that everyone else for the most part is happy and doing well." Grace took a sip of her tea.

Hesitating, April pushed the pastry around on her plate. "Well, I guess I'm glad they're doing okay, but I don't understand why I'm not. I worked hard to put Center Stage Press together, and I think I was fair with everyone."

"How would you define *fair*, dear?"

"Well, I gave John a way out of his writer's block and possible humiliation. Laney got to write her mystery books, and Devon received a higher royalty on his books than he ever would have with Nora."

"So you believe that you were the only option they would have ever had."

"Probably," April replied quickly. "Where else would they have gone?"

"My dear, you would be surprised at the synchronicities awaiting everyone in this life. There is never just one door. You always had choices, too, April. You never had to do the things you did."

"Just what did I do wrong? I was just looking out for myself. No one else is going to do it. In case you haven't noticed, it's a dog-eat-dog world out there. You didn't see Jeffrey Taber worrying about me when his wife got her knickers in a wad, did you? And what about Nora Oliver? She was so ready to use me as an editor at a receptionist's pay, and who was the first person she fired?" April grabbed her pastry and bit off a piece like a dog ripping meat off a bone before slapping it back on the plate.

"I notice you didn't mention Brandon Foster. What did he do to deserve what you did to him?"

April narrowed her eyes, trying to recall if she had seen what happened to Brandon in her recent "travels." Looking at Grace, she said, "I just realized that I never saw what happened to Brandon after I moved to Chicago. Oh, I know that BFI went under, but what happened to him?"

"Are you sure you want to know?" Grace asked. "I deliberately kept that from you because I thought even you might have been crushed by it."

Smirking at Grace's thinly veiled sarcasm, April replied, "I think I can handle it."

"Two years after you destroyed his company—" April started to protest, but Grace raised her hand to forestall her comments. "Two years later, Brandon was so despondent that his wife took his child and left him. She still loved him, but she couldn't watch him rip himself apart."

This time April did interrupt. "Boohoo. My husband left me, too." She had never revealed to anyone that Martin had been the one who asked for a divorce.

"Yes, but you didn't put a gun to your head and blow your brains out."

"Oh, my god! Are you kidding me?" Now she knew why he hadn't been one of those who had so easily trashed her when she was down.

"Why on earth would I kid about something like that? You started a ball rolling that Brandon was not strong enough to stop. You never once considered how your actions would impact him, did you?"

Getting defensive, April snapped, "He was a big boy. It's not my fault that he turned out to be a wuss."

"Certainly, he could have made different choices—"

"See! Not my fault!"

"—but you never considered for one minute what might already have been going on in his head, the insecurities he might have been struggling with — things that made him more vulnerable than usual. No, all you cared about was what you wanted."

"Now wait a minute!" April straightened in her chair, ready for a fight.

"No, April, you wait a minute," Grace barked, more harshly than April expected. "Why do you think you were given the opportunity to review your life before your life had reached its conclusion? It certainly wasn't to make excuses for yourself! You have a chance to make amends for all the ..." Grace paused. "... well, I can't think of a more appropriate word ... for all the shitty things you've done to people in your lifetime.

"You can make the right choice and live a better life, or you can make yet another selfish decision and who knows where it will lead you."

"What are you talking about? What's done is done. I can't change the past, and I don't seem to have much control over my present or my future."

"That's where you're wrong, April." April noticed that Grace was no longer calling her *dear*, and she realized that she missed it.

"You have a chance to make a difference. The Universe is giving you a chance to change one thing in your life that will make your life and everyone else's living in your sphere of influence better. Just remember that everything is connected. If you choose a point early in your life, the paths you walked after that will be different ones.

"This will not be an easy decision, and I will be here to walk you through it. Take some time to think about it. I'll leave you alone for a while, and then we'll talk."

"Wait! Is this for real?" April was still toying with the idea that she was having an unusually lucid dream.

Grace stared at her for a minute. "Was your journey back in time real? How could you possibly know what went on with others when you weren't actually there?"

"LSD?" April replied, groping for a rational explanation.

Grace didn't bother to answer. She just turned and walked away.

April couldn't get her head around the idea that she could change her past. How was that even possible? What would she change? Her first thought was to keep Elisa from finding out about her and Jeffrey. No, better just not to have an affair with him at all. If she could do that, she would still be Vice-President of Dietz & Holcombe, making a seven-figure income. That sounded good, she thought.

At just that moment, Grace returned. "Well, do you have any thoughts?"

"If I could go back to when I was at Dietz & Holcombe and *not* start having an affair with him, his wife wouldn't have anything to find out. I'd still be Vice-President."

"Have you thought this through completely?" Grace asked.

"What's there to think about? If I hadn't gotten fired by Jeffrey, I wouldn't have had to go through all the hard work and heartache of the last two decades."

"Let's see how that would have worked out, okay?"

"Huh?" April muttered just as Grace waved her hand.

This time, April experienced a different timeline, one that was unfamiliar. Instead of running in what almost felt like real time, it was more like a movie trailer. She saw herself in her office at Dietz & Holcombe.

Fast forward to Jeffrey's office with all the executives seated around a conference table. Jeffrey was announcing that Dietz & Holcombe would be filing for bankruptcy, and it was unlikely that a reorganization would pull them out of the hole they were in.

Fast forward to her office. "Jeffrey, what the hell is going on?"

"April, we moved too quickly with the Village Projects. We should have stuck with our original plan, but we got greedy. Now we're drowning in overhead. There's more going out than coming in. I've tried to test the waters to see if we could sell off some of the projects, but the only offers are way under-valued. It wouldn't keep us afloat."

Fast forward to April working as a temp at a concrete plant.

"Stop!" shouted April. Grace obliged. "Is that what would have happened if I had stayed at Dietz & Holcombe?"

"That is pretty much like all the possibilities there. Your ambition and greed would most likely have influenced Jeffrey to stretch himself beyond his normal limits."

"Well, that's crap!"

Grace was not surprised that April had not even thought about the fact that such a choice would have meant she would never have met John and that Hannah would never have been born. She had to admit, however, that she was disappointed. This one might be a tougher nut to crack than she had thought.

"Any other thoughts?" Grace inquired.

Chewing on the inside of her cheek, April thought for a few minutes. "What about Brandon? If I had never introduced him to Jeffrey, he wouldn't be dead."

"Does that matter to you?" Grace asked, finding it difficult at this point to believe that April cared.

"Well, if I hadn't introduced him to Jeffrey, I could have worked my way up in BFI or maybe found something else in Memphis that suited me better."

Grace sighed. She knew it was too good to be true that April was thinking of someone other than herself. Her hope waning, Grace waved her hand.

April was back in Memphis, working as a receptionist at BFI.

Fast forward to six months later when April was being handed her pink slip by Norman Crosswell.

"What do you mean *unsatisfactory performance*?" she demanded. "You can't find a better receptionist than me!"

"That may be true, April, but your unfortunate habit of blackmailing people with information to get what you want is not going to be tolerated any longer. By the way, you should probably not put BFI on your resume because I will not be recommending you for any positions."

Fast forward to April fixing supper for Martin, her ex-husband. Unable to find a job, she had had to move in with Martin. Life had come full circle to the path she was on before she ever met Brandon.

Fast forward to a couple of years later. April was reading the newspaper across from Martin at the breakfast table when she came across an article in the business section.

> Brandon Foster, founder of BFI, was found dead in his home yesterday by his wife, Elisa. Plagued by financial worries and other personal issues, Mr. Foster had been seeing a therapist for nearly a year, according to our sources. At a press conference this morning, his friend and investment advisor, Chad Winston, spoke lovingly of his friend but confirmed that he had been having personal challenges of late. He stressed that even though he and his wife Elisa had supported his efforts to seek help, it seemed that whatever was bothering him was more than he could handle. Such a sad end for a man who was incredibly innovative in business.

Slipping back into the present, April snapped, "I hate to repeat myself, but that's crappy, too! What's the point of changing things in the past if they don't ever work out any better?" The thought of living with Martin again sent a shiver through her body.

"Perhaps you just haven't found the right answer to your

problem," Grace offered.

"That's easy for you to say," April retorted. Grace did not respond.

After a few minutes, April said, "Well, that only leaves the Center Stage Press phase of my life."

"What about your childhood?"

"What about it? I had a mother and father, a brother and a sister. They're all dead, and I don't think any of that was my fault. I can't think of anything I could change there that would make any difference in my life now."

Grace took a big gulp of tea. Perhaps Henry could add a touch of something to her next glass. It was looking as if she might need it. She couldn't help but wonder what had happened to the compassion, the shame, and even the regret that April had felt earlier when she had first seen the visions, real and contrived, with which Grace had teased her before sending her back to relive the actual path she had taken as an adult. Knowing April had to come to a solution more or less on her own, Grace played along. "Okay, so what would you change about the Center Stage Press phase of your life?"

Now that April was certain her problems had not begun with BFI or Dietz & Holcombe, she looked absolutely radiant as she contemplated how to get Center Stage Press up and running again.

Grace could hear her thoughts, and it was all she could do not to reach across the table and shake April until her teeth rattled. It had been centuries since she had encountered anyone this self-absorbed, who saw everything from her own self-focused vantage point. She didn't understand that life was only responding to her selfishness, bringing her what she desired, but not without the price that came along with selfishness.

When April asked Henry for a refill on her tea, it brought Grace's attention back to the question at hand. "So what's next?" Grace asked rather gruffly. April noticed her tone and frowned. She couldn't understand why Grace was upset. After all, it was her life in the balance.

"Well, I'm not sure. It seems that going to work for Nora Oliver has to stay the same as does bringing John and Laney and Devon into the fold. Perhaps if I had not let myself get involved with John—" Grace snorted.

"What?" April demanded. Grace glared at her. April raised her eyebrows and shook her head questioningly at Grace.

Grace lost it. "For cripes' sake, woman, don't you realize that if you hadn't gotten involved with John, you would never have had Hannah?"

For a brief moment, April felt that odd sensation she had felt before leaving Chicago. It seemed so long ago that she had forgotten about it. *How old would Hannah be now*, she wondered. *Eighteen this year*, she realized after some quick calculation. She had probably graduated from high school in May. *I wonder what she looks like. The spitting image of John probably.*

Grace was silent. This was a start. At least she was unselfishly thinking about someone else.

"You're right, Grace. That wouldn't be fair to Hannah or to John. He truly loves her."

"What about you? Don't you love her?"

The question shook April. It had been so long since love had been a part of her life that she didn't think she could answer the question. "I don't know what I feel for her. She hasn't been a part of my life for a decade."

"Be honest, April. She hasn't really been a part of your life since the day she was born."

April flinched. Put that way, it made her sound like a real bitch. "She hasn't wanted to be a part of my life either," she said defensively. "I tried to call her for a month before I left Chicago, and she wouldn't return my calls."

"So, after not being there for her for fifteen years at that point, you were expecting her to run into your arms and forgive you?" Despite her reluctance, April was beginning to see Hannah's point of view. Grace continued, "Being a mother means that you can't think only of yourself, April. Actually, being a good person means that you have to put yourself in the other person's shoes so that you have a balanced view of any situation."

Trying to regain control of the situation and avoid answering Grace's question, April said, "Okay, so not getting involved with John is off the table." Grace rolled her eyes. April ignored her.

"I'm stumped. If I choose not to go to work for Nora Oliver, then I would probably never have thought about starting my own press. If I hadn't met John there and convinced him to sign with Center Stage, we would probably never have gotten involved. Besides, without his name starting out, I don't know that I could have accomplished what I did. Plus, you just got through telling me that *not* hooking up with John was a bad idea."

Grace tried to maintain her poise, but she was weakening.

"So," April continued, "the only other thing would be how I set up the contracts with my other authors, but I have to tell you that I'm not sure that would have made a difference fifteen years down the road from when I started. Eventually, they would all have been able to leave. John is evidence that you can't tie someone to you forever, no matter how hard you try."

"Your daughter may have come to that same conclusion about *you*," remarked Grace.

April didn't respond. Thinking about Hannah stirred up a myriad of emotions, all of which were disconcerting. Instead she looked out the windows of the deck to the far bank of the river. On the other side, a small boy was fishing off the bank. She hadn't noticed him earlier. *What is he doing out there alone?* she wondered. *He could easily fall in, and the current is swift.*

Grace watched April's concern for the boy. Her hopes for April tingled, showing some signs of life again. Grace saw the boy's father walk out of the thick mix of bushes and spindly trees growing along the bank.

April jerked forward in her chair. *Watch out!* she cried out to the boy in her head, thinking he was in danger of being attacked. Grace's hopes soared. She was actually showing concern for someone else, even though misguided.

The boy's father patted the boy on his shoulder. Looking up at the man, the boy grinned before jumping up, grabbing his fishing pole, and taking his dad's hand. As they walked downriver together, April felt envious. At first she thought it was just the reaction to being wrong, but quickly realized it was more than that. She sensed a desire for what the boy's father obviously had — unconditional love — but she didn't know what to do about it.

Her thoughts wandered back to things Grace had said about her when they first arrived. She hadn't wanted to believe they were true.

Grace held her breath, anxious for April to take the next step.

April finally spoke. "Grace, earlier you said that I had taken such promise and twisted it and distorted it until in the end, I was more damaged than the people I betrayed. Did you mean that?" Elbows on the table, April rested her chin on her hands, and waited.

"Sadly, I did, dear." Grace winced at the words. It seemed that not all the pain was to be endured by April. "But," she continued, "it doesn't mean that you can't still live up to the promise of your life."

Thoughtful, April turned her head, continuing to rest it on her hands, and gazed out at the river. She felt different, tired almost. A part of her wanted to let her eyes close and ignore all these new feelings, to just go back to her bed and let the rest of her life pass in a fog. Even though she sometimes craved her manic times, she had found out recently, thanks to Andrea Greene, that life was not being as accommodating as it had once been. She was going to have to rethink her approach to her life because she was feeling very much analog in a digital world.

Turning back toward Grace, April hesitated, trying to find the right words. Grace smiled in anticipation. "I'm starting to think that the problem with my life is me."

Not wanting to push too hard, Grace asked, "When you say that you're the problem, what does that mean to you? Are you looking back and feeling sorry for yourself or are you talking about something else?" Grace nervously straightened the straps of her pinafore. The energy was building. They were so close.

Running her tongue across her upper lip, April swallowed and sat quietly before answering. "I never really thought that I was betraying anyone. I believed that everyone would do the same to me unless I did it first. I always viewed life as a game so it's always been about winning and losing. Just because I won and someone else lost didn't qualify it as a betrayal.

"Before you arrived this morning, I was wondering where everyone in my life had gone. I think perhaps now I understand, at least a little."

"Dear, do you remember how I described the nature of your name while we were at your house?"

"Not really. I was still a little fuzzy at that point and wondering what a nutcase was doing in my kitchen." Grace laughed, glad to see that April's sense of humor was still intact.

"Well, I told you that April means *to open* like the opening of flowers. Remember, flowers open themselves up, giving of themselves to the world and taking from it only what they need to allow their beauty to shine forth. It is a perfect give and take. Where do you think you have gotten off track in expressing the nature of your name?"

April tugged on the end of her nose and stared at the table top. "I suppose I've been more interested in taking what I want than in the giving."

Despite its being unorthodox for one in her position, Grace clapped. "Oh, my dear, just by seeing that one thing, you have turned a corner in your life."

"I'm feeling a little overwhelmed, to be honest," admitted April.

Grace knew how hard it was to face one's demons and admit that they had been the source of your unhappiness or your failures. These demons had normally been a part of one's life for so long that they felt familiar and safe — nothing out of the ordinary.

"I'm not surprised. Would you like to walk along the river for a bit — just to clear your head?" Grace asked.

"That sounds wonderful!" April was surprised by her own eagerness.

Grace motioned to Henry that they would return as she led the way out the back stairs from the deck down to the path along the river. They walked in silence for a while. April sneezed.

"Oh dear! Are you allergic?" Grace asked.

"No. I must have breathed some dust up my nose." Spying an old wooden bench much in need of paint along the river walk, she asked, "If it will hold us both, would you like to sit for a few minutes and watch the river?"

Grace readily agreed. It was important for April to feel like she was more in control of her life than she had been for the last several hours. They sat quietly for a while. Grace could hear the thoughts going through April's head. Fortunately, April seemed to have forgotten about Grace's talent. Although there was a great deal of chaos, a thread of understanding was beginning to weave its way through, pulling April out of the discord into clarity.

Without warning, Grace sneezed, which was highly irregular. She assumed that the Universe had a reason or was just enjoying itself. "Are you allergic?" asked April, a slight giggle escaping.

Grace laughed. "No. I just think the Universe is having a laugh at my expense."

April started to laugh, and it escalated until tears were flowing down her face, which only made it worse. Finally, when all the negative energy that had been tethering her had loosened its grip, she literally collapsed against the back of the bench. "I don't think I've ever laughed so hard, and I don't even know what was so funny."

"That was grace," her companion stated.

"You?"

Graced laughed, realizing what she had said. "No, I meant the grace of God, being in God's favor. It was a gift that released you from the grip of your own negativity. Joy in the form of laughter is a pure emotion. When it flows through you from Spirit, it sweeps away all the things the world around you has taught you are true, but are not. The experience gives you a taste of joy, and your desire for it can overwhelm any feelings of anger or disappointment or envy or sadness."

April inhaled deeply, feeling a sense of freedom that was unfamiliar to her, but as comforting as a warm blanket on a frigid evening. "Why?" she asked.

"Why what?" responded Grace.

"Why couldn't I see what I was doing to the people around me? Why was I so blinded?" Grace felt a twinge in her heart looking at the expression on April's face.

"Sweetheart," Grace began. April smiled at the warm endearment. "The answer lies in the name you chose for your publishing company."

"Center Stage?"

"Exactly. When you're standing at center stage and all the spotlights are shining down on you, what can you see?"

April thought for a moment. "I guess you wouldn't be able to see anything except for the glare of the lights all around you."

"And that's my point. When you insist on living your life at center stage, for all practical purposes, you're all alone. You are so blinded by the spotlights that you can't see those around you. They are almost like figments of your imagination, so how can they have feelings or dreams? The spotlights become blinders, freeing you from the need to give, the need to care about others, the need to love anyone but yourself."

Tears were rolling down April's cheeks. "Oh, Grace, I'm fifty-one years old, and I've screwed up my whole life!" She buried her head against Grace's shoulder.

"It's never too late, dear. That's what this is all about."

Sniffling, she raised her head. "I don't see how. My daughter hates me. John would probably cross the street if he saw me coming. I don't have a business. Hell, I tried to buy a business a little over a year ago, and the woman told me to get out of her store! It's no use. Too little, too late."

Turning sideways on the bench, Grace grabbed April firmly by the shoulders. "After all we've been through together, I'm not going to sit here and listen to you feel sorry for yourself! Is that all you've learned?" She couldn't resist shaking her just a bit.

"Well, what am I supposed to do? I'm fresh out of answers."

"Don't ask yourself what the old April would do. Ask yourself what the new April would do, the one who wants to love and be loved, the one who cares what happens to other people and how they feel. Do you love your daughter?"

April knew she hadn't been able to answer that question earlier, but now she realized that she did love her. She had never realized it until now, perhaps because she had never believed that Hannah would love her back. Even now, she wasn't sure.

"Risk it," said Grace.

April jumped. "Sheesh! I forgot you can hear my thoughts."

Ignoring her comment, Grace said, "Well? Are you going to risk it?"

"What should I do?"

Grace wanted to be able to tell her exactly what she should do, but she knew she couldn't. "I can't tell you that, April. You have to make that decision on your own. You are the one who has to be comfortable with your decision, not me. All I will say is that you should be careful not to slip into your old comfort zones. Don't choose to run rather than face your demons."

April looked into Grace's eyes, feeling like she had known this woman forever rather than a few hours. "I think I understand. I don't know what I'm going to do yet, but I won't let you down."

Grace smiled. "Just don't let yourself down, dear. That's the most important thing." Glancing at the setting sun, Grace said, "Well, I think it's time we call it a day."

Chapter 32

New Beginnings

April arrived home just before the sun disappeared from the sky. Grace stepped out of the car. April walked around the car and gave her a warm hug.

"Thank you for everything, Grace. I'll never be able to pay you back for what you've done for me. Don't be a stranger, okay?"

Grace laughed. "No need, and don't worry. I'll be keeping an eye on you," she replied as she turned toward the sidewalk. April stopped on the porch to watch Grace walking down the street. When she turned into the driveway of the fourth house down, April opened her front door and entered her house.

She went into the kitchen where she saw that Grace had cleaned up before they left. Strangely, the muffin basket was sitting in the middle of the table and was overflowing with muffins. How was that possible? She had eaten two muffins herself this morning. Thinking of Grace, however, April wasn't sure that anything was impossible.

After starting the coffee pot brewing, she went into the living room and pulled a packet of stationery and a legal pad out of the writing desk. On the way back to the house from The Crossroads, she had decided that making amends with Hannah was the place to start if she wanted to turn her life around. Since she hadn't been able to contact her by phone, she thought a letter was the next best option. Returning to the kitchen, she fixed a cup of coffee and sat down at the table.

Her pen poised above the yellow paper of the legal pad, she waited for inspiration. Where should she start? How could she begin to explain the last ten years, or as Grace had so quickly pointed out, the last eighteen years? She didn't want to make excuses. First of all, Hannah was too smart to accept such a weak approach. Besides, as she had reluctantly recognized today, there were no adequate excuses.

Remembering Grace's words, she tried to tune into the new April, the one open to love and to being loved and to caring about what happened to other people and how they felt. As she embraced this new self, she began to write.

Dear Hannah,

I am hopeful you will read this letter, but I will understand if you cannot bring yourself to do so.

There are no excuses for my behavior regarding you for the last eighteen years. To be truthful, there is no excuse for my behavior for the last fifty-one years. I have been so busy trying to win at life that I never understood what I was actually losing. So many wonderful opportunities have come into my life, but I could never see them the way I should have because I was blinded by my need to be center stage. I know this does not make up for what I have done to you, but I still have to say that I am grateful you have such a loving father. Unfortunately, I betrayed him as well.

When I look back over my life (and believe me when I say that I have had an eye-opening experience in that area recently), I realize how many people I have hurt. I also realize that I was never the winner. I have without fail been the loser all my life. Don't jump to conclusions. I am not asking for your pity. I don't deserve anyone's pity because I am totally responsible for the mess I call my life and for the carnage I have left behind. The only thing that soothes my pain somewhat is that those I hurt the most had a better sense of themselves than I and managed to manifest a better life for themselves, despite me.

I know that I cannot make up for the time we have lost, and I know that it might be impossible for you to ever love me as your mother. However, I am pleading for a chance to see you and to prove to you that I am not the same person I was.

I don't ever expect John or Laney or Devon to forgive me. I plowed through their lives with no regard for their needs so I can't expect absolution from them. I shouldn't expect it from you either, but for the first time, I realize how much I do love you and how afraid I've always been that you could never love me. I hid that weakness from myself by concentrating on staying center stage. I am truly sorry.

I don't know what else to say, so if you feel you could meet me for dinner, send me a note, and I will fly up immediately.

Sincerely, April

After copying the letter onto stationery, April folded it and placed it into an envelope. She had no problem knowing where to send it since John and Hannah were still living in the condo she had when they first met. Placing a stamp on the envelope, she decided to walk down to the corner mailbox before she lost her nerve. Grabbing up the legal pad sheet, she hurried out the door. After posting the letter, she stopped at the house where Grace lived. She wanted to show her letter to her and see what she thought. Knocking on the door, a young woman with a small child on her hip answered the door. *Grace never mentioned living with her daughter*, April thought.

"Uh, is Grace home?" she asked.

"Who?" the young woman looked confused.

"Grace. An older woman. She dresses kind of old-fashioned. She rode into town with me this morning, and I saw her come up this driveway after she left my house."

The woman shrugged. "She doesn't live here. I'm sorry."

Distressed, April said, "Do you know of an older woman who lives in one of the nearby houses?"

"I've never seen anyone fitting your description. Most of the people around me are young with children."

Nodding, April turned to leave as the woman closed the front door. Where did Grace go? She had seen her go up that driveway. She hadn't actually seen her go in though. By this time, April had reached her front door. Feeling antsy, she wanted to talk to Grace. Walking into the kitchen, she laid the sheet of paper with her initial draft of Hannah's letter on the table. Heading for the coffee pot to fortify herself with caffeine, she caught sight of a folded piece of paper next to the muffins that had mysteriously appeared earlier.

Picking it up, she read: *April, trust yourself. You are on the right track. You don't have to find me. I am always here, watching over you, but you need to be strong. Make decisions from the right vantage point, and you'll be all right.*

By the way, the letter you wrote to Hannah was wonderful.

April's tears fell onto the note.

****

The fourth of July was in two days, and April had not heard from Hannah. It had been a week, plenty of time to have received an answer if there was going to be one. April knew that she couldn't allow herself to slip back into her recent patterns of ignoring things and hoping they would go away so she wouldn't have to deal with them. She had to take the initiative. She had to see Hannah, even if it was from a distance.

The condo association where she had once lived had always had a 4th of July bash on the roof deck of the building where they could watch fireworks in all directions. She knew that John and Hannah always attended because she had been invited several times years ago, but declined. Even though Hannah was nearly eighteen now, she believed she would still spend the holiday with John and their friends. This was her chance. Making reservations for a flight out the next morning, she quickly packed. Not knowing what would happen, she prepared for the best and packed for a week.

Arriving in Chicago the next day, she hailed a cab and went straight to her hotel, picked because it was the closest to her old condo building. After unpacking, she called downstairs to the salon and made an appointment. It had been a long time since her hair had been styled. Perhaps she could get some highlights put in it. John had always loved her hair, but these days the gray was starting to show.

Sitting in the salon, waiting for her hair to dry, she felt equal amounts of excitement and dread building. In an irrational moment, she had agreed to let the stylist cut her hair. The young woman had said it would make her look younger. She wasn't sure that Hannah would care, but she realized she wanted it for herself. She wanted to look like a new person to go along with how she was feeling inside.

"Time to make you beautiful," declared the stylist as she turned off the dryer. Her hair was still slightly damp when the stylist began using a brush and a hand dryer to shape her hair into a new style. April closed her eyes. Better to wait for the finished product. She had never worn short hair.

"Voilà!" the stylist announced as she turned April around to face the mirror.

"Oh, my god!" cried April.

"What's the matter?" The stylist quickly went from pleased to wary.

"Who is that woman?" April asked.

Laughing, the stylist said, "You, ten years younger, maybe even fifteen."

"I absolutely love it!" April's hair was very thick so the short cut would be easy to maintain without having to use a curling iron. Getting up from the chair, she walked to the triple mirror and twirled around. It was amazing, but she actually felt lighter. Over-tipping the woman, she rushed out of the salon with the intention of buying a new dress for tomorrow. She didn't remember ever feeling this alive.

By the time the day drew to a close, April was so excited she didn't know if she would be able to sleep, but when her head hit the pillow, she slept like a newborn baby.

The next day April walked around, wanting to see what she had left behind with new eyes. As she passed the condo building, she stopped. This had been her refuge when she left Dietz & Holcombe and her sanctuary when she worked for Nora Oliver. Then it had become the place she had avoided as much as possible after Hannah was born until finally, she was exiled from it. She hoped it wouldn't be forever.

Walking on, she came to the office building where her life had started down a road that eventually led to her fall. Of course, she thought, it had ultimately led her to this moment, and for this, she was grateful even if she didn't know what would happen with Hannah. Looking up, she could remember how she had felt the first time the sign for Center Stage Press was lit. In her mind, she could still see the green glow it had cast, letting the world know she was a mover-and-shaker. Now she wasn't even sure what that meant.

She walked down to the edge of Lake Michigan and watched the waves as they rolled in, sometimes dumping flotsam on the sand, and then slipping back into the lake, only to rush ashore to repeat the process. Watching the steady rhythm, she realized how easy it was to fall into old patterns of behavior, thinking things were improving each time, when in truth, it was just more of the same. Only the people and circumstances were different, and sometimes, like the waves, you left debris behind. Turning back toward the street, she knew that she had changed, but she also knew it wasn't going to be easy.

By the time nine o'clock rolled around, April had put on all three dresses she had bought the day before. Finally settling on her favorite, the amber-colored, sleeveless, silk dress with a low-cut neckline, she accessorized with gold earrings and a matching necklace. Her low-heeled shoes looked like they had been made for the dress. When she saw them yesterday, she hailed it as a good omen. Rather than take a cab, she decided to walk the short distance to the condos.

The doorman nodded to her as she walked into the building. She doubted that he remembered her so he must think she was here for the party. Stepping into the elevator, she took a deep breath as it began to rise toward the roof. "I hope you're with me, Grace," she whispered. She felt a small puff of air brush her cheek. Since it would be highly unusual to catch a breeze in an elevator, she could only believe that it was Grace. "Thanks," she whispered just before the elevator doors opened.

There was a small lobby outside the elevator before you reached the roof access. April hesitated. Her insides were quivering. She didn't know if it was fear or excitement. She was alone in the foyer so she moved to the glass exit door and peered out into the crowd on the roof. The music was competing to be heard with the voices of the party-goers. The elevator bell dinged, and April stepped to the side of the door. A couple walked out of the elevator and smiled at April as they pushed open the door. At that moment, she caught a glimpse of John with his arm around someone, but she couldn't see her face. As the crowd shifted, she saw her. It was Hannah. She was so beautiful that it took her breath away. She and John looked like they had been created by the same artist.

April couldn't bring herself to walk through the door. A man pulled the roof door open, waiting for his significant other to walk through. As she reached him, she stopped and kissed him on the lips lightly. The movement and the light from the lobby area shining out onto the roof caught John's eye. There, just inside the doorway, he saw a woman who brought back such powerful feelings that his gut clenched and his breath caught. Momentarily distracted by his reaction, he quickly returned his gaze to the doorway, but she was gone.

"Sweetheart," he said to Hannah, "would you keep Laney and Devon company for a few minutes? I want to check on something."

"Sure, Dad!" Hannah had loved these 4th of July parties since she was a kid. Of course, people had come and gone in the building, but there were still a lot of the old crowd remaining, and the new crowd was pretty cool. She had noticed in the last couple of years that the music was starting to reflect the younger age range of the residents. She was rocking back and forth to the music when Devon asked her to dance. She readily accepted. Devon might be older, but he didn't seem to know it.

John walked to the roof door and peered into the lobby area. No one. Turning around, he scanned the crowd. He knew a lot of them. Some had brought guests, and he didn't always know who were newer residents and who were guests. Perhaps the woman he had seen was a guest. He was sure that if she lived in the building, he would have noticed her. There! He spotted her watching the dance floor. Her back was to him, but there was no mistaking that it was the same woman. Feeling incredibly awkward since he had not approached a women like this in years, he moved slowly toward her until he could reach out and touch her.

"Ahem," he cleared his throat. "Do I know you?" he asked as he reached out to touch her shoulder. She turned and looked at him. The spotlights on the roof shone directly on her face. As his heart leaped into his throat, he knew there was no mistake. The same golden hair and the same flecks of gold in her eyes.

"Hello, John," she said. Her heart was racing, but she tried to remain outwardly calm.

"April, what a surprise! You look … well, you look even better than you did twenty years ago, if that's possible."

"You, too," she stammered. "I mean, you've gotten even better-looking with age."

Still in a mild state of shock at seeing his ex-wife after so many years, John couldn't think of anything except "Did Hannah know you were coming?"

"No, I never heard back from her. I'm guessing that you know about the letter?"

"Yes, she showed it to me. I thought she was going to write you back. We talked about it, and she seemed ready to deal with the past." He seemed uncertain about where to go next with the conversation.

"It's all right, John. I have no intention of causing you or Hannah any problems. If she doesn't want to see me, it's okay. I just wanted to see her," she said, looking back toward the dance floor. "She's a gorgeous young woman, John, and she seems very happy. You've obviously done a wonderful job."

Turning her attention back to John, she said, " I don't know how to explain what has happened to me except to say that it was something extraordinary, and it has made me see my life and others differently." She paused. "I don't want to intrude in your life, but I want to say that I treated you badly. I used you. I realize now that I did love you, but I couldn't see beyond myself far enough to share that feeling with you or even acknowledge it.

"When I told Hannah in my letter that I realized that I had always been so focused on winning that I never understood what I was losing, you were one of the two most important things I lost in my life, Hannah being the other."

John was overwhelmed. He had pushed April out of his mind and his heart so long ago. At least he had thought so. Now that she was standing in front of him without the anger and the callousness, the spark that had always been there for her was starting to flare into a flame. He fought it. How could he take the chance? He couldn't let Hannah be hurt again. All he could do was stare into April's eyes. His heart wanted to say one thing and his head another, which resulted in his being voiceless.

April picked up the conversational thread that had been left dangling. "It's been great seeing you, John. Would you tell Hannah that I think she is the most beautiful young woman I have ever seen? Also, I saw that Laney and Devon are with you tonight. Can you tell them that I am so sorry for the way I treated them and that I'm very happy for their success?" John nodded. "I won't bother you again." With that, she raised up on her toes and pecked him on the cheek before walking back toward the elevator.

Laney walked up beside John. "Was that who I think it was?"

Swallowing hard and fighting tears, John said, "Yeah, it was."

"What did she want?"

"She just wanted to see Hannah and to tell me and you and Devon how sorry she was for how she treated us."

"Humph! That doesn't sound like the April I knew."

John gazed toward the roof access door. "I don't think it was the April we knew."

Hannah walked off the dance floor with Devon, laughing at something he had said. Alarmed when she saw the twisted expression on her dad's face, she cried, "What's wrong? Has something happened?"

Before John could answer, Laney said, "Your mother was here."

Bristling, she said, "What did she do?"

Reaching out to put his arm around his daughter, John said, "She didn't do anything, sweetheart, except apologize to all of us. She just wanted to see you, and she asked me to tell you that you are the most beautiful young woman she has ever seen."

Hannah looked at him. "Then why are you so upset?"

"I just had a glimpse of what might have been, and I experienced such a tremendous sense of loss that it felt like my heart was being ripped from my chest."

"Oh, Daddy. You still love her after all these years, don't you?" John just looked at his daughter. She was voicing the feeling that he had been afraid to face. "Go find her. I didn't write her back because I was afraid it would upset you to see her again, but I do want to see her. I never dreamed you still loved her."

John hesitated. "Go!" said Laney. "Life's too short to not explore every opportunity." John rushed toward the elevator.

April had reached the ground floor. The doorman held the door for her. She stepped outside but was unable to make a decision about where to go. She hadn't actually thought beyond the point of seeing Hannah. Obviously, it was too much to hope that she could ever be a part of their lives again. Tears flowed down her face. The doorman offered her a handkerchief, which she gratefully accepted. Patting her face dry and handing the handkerchief back, she asked him, "Do you remember me?"

"Yes, ma'am, I do. I have to say that you seem a lot different though."

"Well, I cut my hair short," she replied.

"No, ma'am, that's not it. You seem softer somehow."

That was all it took. She reached for his handkerchief again as she sobbed in earnest.

"April! What's wrong?" John rushed out the front door and pulled her into his arms as if the last decade had never happened.

April allowed herself to melt into his arms. If it was only temporary, she wanted to have the memory of it.

"Why are you crying?" he insisted.

"Oh, John, my whole world has changed in such a short time. I'm not the same person I was even a week ago, but I'm not sure if it will make a difference. I've been told by a very wise woman that it will, but when I looked at you and Hannah, I knew that I could never come close to recovering what I threw away so carelessly." She laid her head on his shoulder and sobbed some more.

Taking a deep breath before plunging into unknown waters, John said, "April, I have always loved you. I haven't always liked you." He heard her hiccup. "When I saw you tonight, my heart nearly jumped out of my chest. Talking to you, I met the person I had always loved but rarely saw. I've never wanted to hurt you, and neither does Hannah. She just told me that she hadn't written you back because she thought it would upset me, but that she really does want to see you."

April pulled her head back and looked up at him. "Did she really? Are you sure she's not just trying to please you? I couldn't stand it if I created any more chaos in your lives."

Pulling her close, he said quietly, "Let's just take it slowly. You can get to know Hannah one day at a time, and we'll see where it goes from there." Laughing, he said, "However, when it comes to Laney and Devon, you're on your own. I have absolutely no control over either one of them, especially Laney."

April laughed, remembering how bold and saucy Laney had been when they first met. She was around seventy-five now, and April doubted that she had mellowed.

They headed back inside. April felt hope surge through her body. Perhaps there was salvation, even for her.

Chapter 33

Two years later

Sitting idly at her computer, April glanced out her window. She didn't have the view of Lake Michigan that she had had once. Rather than being able to watch the motion of the waves, now she watched children playing in the small park across the street. Surprisingly, she found it quite soothing. Two years ago, with the encouragement of Hannah and John, she had sold her Mississippi home and returned to Chicago. She was able to find a work-at-home job as an editor for an online news site. It wasn't a huge salary, but if she carefully managed the money she already had, her salary would cover the expense of her one-bedroom condo. Since she didn't have to drive to work, the expense of fuel and clothing was substantially reduced.

The big plus of her job was that she had a considerable amount of freedom. She worked much faster than most and purposely never turned in her projects until just before the deadline. She was well aware that if her employers thought she could do twice the work for the same pay, they would be more than glad to create a new performance level for her. Although she enjoyed her work, her job was just that: a job. Her life was the time she spent with John and Hannah.

In less than an hour, she was supposed to meet them at the condo. It seemed that Hannah had a big announcement, and she wanted everybody, including Laney and Devon, to be there. For the last two years, Hannah had been attending a community college nearby where her focus was on writing. After returning to Chicago, April had discovered that Hannah finished a novel when she was fifteen. According to John, she rewrote it three times before she was satisfied. He had offered to show it to Nora Oliver, but Hannah declined. She said she wanted to be sure that she had what it took to be a writer before taking that step. What that meant, John had confided to April, he didn't exactly know.

After the short drive to the condo, April stood outside John's door. She could hear Laney and the others guffawing about something. The moment seemed very surreal to her even though she had been around them all for the last two years. Every day she was grateful for Grace, wherever she was. If not for her, this would never have been a path she could have travelled down. She knew she could never recapture the times she had lost, but at least she had the chance to love and be loved now. Shaking off the strangeness of the moment, she knocked and then twisted the knob.

"Mom!' Hannah called out. "We've been waiting on you!"

April never stopped feeling blessed every time Hannah called her Mom. "Am I late?" she asked, looking at her watch.

"No, but you know how this bunch is. Tell them the bar will be open and snacks provided, and you better get out of the way." Hannah put her arm around April and kissed her on the cheek.

"Okay, enough drinking and carousing! Everyone take a seat," Hannah ordered. John grinned and escorted April to the sofa. Laney and Devon each plopped down in a chair while Hannah stood center stage, waiting for them to settle down.

"I have an announcement," she said.

Before she could continue, Laney muttered, "Duh!" Hannah smiled at her always feisty "grandmother."

"As you all know, I have been studying at the community college, taking advantage of their excellent writing curriculum—"

"Tell us something we don't know," Devon said.

Hannah laughed. "I don't know why I thought the bunch of you would sit quietly and let me tell you my news."

John spoke up. "Okay, people, as master of this house, I insist on everyone staying mum until Hannah finishes her speech."

"Thanks, Dad. Anyway, I have learned that I can perform under pressure, which was my concern before going into this program. I have done very well in the program, so well in fact that I've been offered an internship with a publishing house in New York."

There was stunned silence. Hannah stood there awkwardly,

waiting. Although April didn't want to see Hannah leave after just having her in her life for two years, she knew she had to put her own feelings aside. "Hannah, that is absolutely wonderful! I can't imagine a better opportunity for you or a better intern for them. I just know this is the doorway to whatever life you choose."

Crying, Hannah rushed into her mother's arms. April hugged her for a moment before holding her at arm's length. "We need to make a toast to your success!" Rolling her eyes toward Laney and Devon, she said, "After that, I think we need to cut those two off." Hannah laughed before running to get a glass for the toast.

John watched his ex-wife and his daughter together. *If only* ... He shook himself. The past was gone. There was only now, but he had to admit that the transformation he had seen in both April and Hannah the last two years had been astounding. He had to admit he wasn't unaffected either. April had never been willing to tell him what had happened with her. She would only say that she had been saved by the grace of God, which had seemed strange coming from April.

****

Three weeks later, Hannah's family, extended family, and lots of friends went to the airport to see her off to New York. There were tears, of course, but no one could tell if they were tears of joy for her bright future or tears of sorrow for the light that wouldn't be in their lives as much.

As soon as the plane took off, April looked at her watch. "Anyone interested in getting some lunch?"

Laney and Devon begged off, both claiming to be at critical points in their writing, which April thought was strange. Looking at John, she raised an eyebrow. "You, too?"

"Oh, no, I'm free all this week," he grinned.

Laughing, she replied, "I don't think it will take us that long to eat."

"You never know," he said, taking her arm and leading her toward the exit.

Lunch was spectacular. John had chosen his favorite restaurant —

his favorite, he said, because of the atmosphere. April had to agree. There were indoor fountains and plants galore. It was like eating in a greenhouse without the humidity.

As they sat drinking coffee, April sighed.

"What's wrong?" John asked.

"Absolutely nothing," she replied. "I just never dreamed I would hear my daughter call me Mom and tell me she would miss me." A tear slipped down her face. "I also never dreamed I would be sitting across from you again as friends."

Looking at her, John started to speak but hesitated. April could tell there was something on his mind. She'd had the feeling all during lunch that he had something to say. Concerned he might not want their relationship to continue now that Hannah was gone, she sat very still, her hands around her coffee cup, waiting for him to speak.

Finally, he leaned forward and took her hands in his. "How would you like to move to the country?"

Startled, she said, "What?"

"You. Me. Move to country." She just stared at him, trying to process what was happening. "I love you, April. I always have. Since you returned two years ago, the *what might have been* that I had always imagined for us has been coming true. I want to take it to the next step if you want to go with me."

Her heart pounding, April closed her eyes and whispered, "Thank you, Grace," as a small puff of air brushed her face.

"Who's Grace?"

"Never mind. I'll explain someday." Pulling his hands to her lips, she kissed them gently. "I would go with you anywhere, John."

About The Author

Dannye Williamsen

I hope you enjoyed *Center Stage.* If you haven't read my other novels, be sure to check them out at this URL: www.amazon.com/Dannye-Williamsen/e/B004KEAFE8 or through the Direct Links below.

www.DannyeWilliamsen.com, www.WilliamsenPublications.com, www.amazon.com, www.SassyScribblers.com

Fiction:

Second Chances:
http://www.amazon.com/Second-Chances-Dannye-Williamsen/dp/097260586X
The Threads That Bind:
http://www.amazon.com/Threads-That-Bind-Dannye-Williamsen/dp/0972605878
Center Stage:
http://www.amazon.com/Center-Stage-Dannye-Williamsen/dp/0972605835
Brita Madison series:
Book 1 – Chasing Shadows
http://www.amazon.com/Chasing-Shadows-Madison-Paranormal-Mysteries/dp/1507743491
Book 2 - Shattered Hearts
https://www.amazon.com/Shattered-Hearts-Madison-Paranormal-Mystery/dp/1542366259
Book 3 - Unraveling memories
https://www.amazon.com/Unraveling-Memories-Madison-Paranormal-Mysteries-ebook/dp/B07T91CWHC
Circles of Freedom:
https://www.amazon.com/Circles-Freedom-Dannye-Williamsen/dp/1719178305
When the Walls Come Tumbling Down:
https://www.amazon.com/When-Walls-Come-Tumbling-Down/dp/B08LNJL1PH
The Elyrian Emergence:

https://www.amazon.com/Elyrian-Emergence-Dannye-Williamsen-ebook/dp/B092P8XQXR

Invisible Shadows:

https://www.amazon.com/Invisible-Shadows-Dannye-Williamsen-ebook/dp/B0B1VV87TT

Nonfiction:

12-Step Business Plan for the Solopreneur

http://www.amazon.com/12-Step-Business-Plan-Solopreneur/dp/1453611223

The Seasons of My Soul – A Poetic Diary

http://www.amazon.com/The-Seasons-My-Soul-Poetic/dp/0972605843

The Creative Model for the Solopreneur – Making the Creative Process Work for You

http://www.amazon.com/The-Creative-Model-Solopreneur-Process/dp/1466262079

Metaphysical Minute – Philosophy on the Run

http://www.williamsenpublications.com/store/p3/_Metaphysical_Minute_-_Philosophy_on_the_Run.html

Life Untwisted - Targeting Your Potential With A Fearless Attitude

http://www.amazon.com/Life-Untwisted-Targeting-Potential-Fearless/dp/0972605851/

MindSlap! - Shifting Your Perspective From Conditioned Reactions To Conscious Choices

http://www.amazon.com/MindSlap-Perspective-Conditioned-Reactions-Conscious/dp/1516815041/

Where Do I Go from Here?

https://www.amazon.com/Where-Do-Go-Here-Consider/dp/1542692520

Book of Metanoia

http://www.amazon.com/Book-Metanoia-Wisdom-Facilitate-Journey-ebook/dp/B00VPJG06I/

A Weary Traveler

https://www.amazon.com/dp/B07T7VGJFQ/

Descriptions of My Fiction Books

Second Chances – Paranormal Suspense

Second Chances is the evolutionary journey of Fredrika, whose life has been defined by her fear of an unspoken power within her and her need to suppress it by controlling herself and the world around her. Everything is brought into question by the appearance of a ghostly stalker, who disrupts her ordered existence and kills her assistant, leaving her clueless how to get rid of the chaos that has taken over her life.

When she is forced to step outside the rational confines of her life to accept the help of a wolf named Avatar, who seems to know more about what's going on than she does, the first step in her evolution begins.

The Threads That Bind – Paranormal Suspense

Thirty-nine years after *Second Chances*, the threads that bind the generations begin to reconnect for the final battle in *The Threads That Bind*. By quirk of fate, Mandy Gray, whose last and best friend was Fredrika Marsh, leaves her secluded profession as a research psychologist in 2019 to take a position as a guidance counselor at Briarton Academy where the orphaned and wealthy Jillian Missildine is a student. They become fast friends, but it is four years before they discover the thread that connects them.

Once this connection is made, all the others — those connected to the past through Freddie and her nemesis — flow swiftly toward each other. The patterns of their lives become tangled and knotted, and the decision has to be made about who will survive.

Center Stage –Romance with a Paranormal Twist

April Saunders is a woman after the brass ring and willing to do whatever it takes to feel it within her grasp. In her quest to be center stage, she barely even notices the trail of victims she leaves in her wake. Eventually her husband and daughter join all the others left behind.

Now the tide has turned. She has been left behind. No power. No options. No family. No friends. No hope.

Then a mysterious and seemingly magical woman named Grace appears at her door. Despondent, April is so weak-willed at this point she allows Grace to take charge, unaware that her life is about to take a turn few ever get to experience. As she takes a preternatural journey into her past, will her ambition continue to rule her heart? *Can there be salvation for one who has betrayed so many?*

Brita Madison Paranormal Mysteries Series

"Only the living are so persistent. The dead seem to understand that time is no longer an issue for them."

Chasing Shadows [Book 1]

Brita Madison is at best a reluctant psychic, and Chief of Police James Weston is the "poster boy for conservative." *Can he accept the unimaginable?*

Brita has found a sanctuary in Williams, Arizona, a refuge from the multitude of visions and voices that have chased her all her life. Then one vision touches her soul, and she finds herself embroiled in the middle of a missing person's case with a woman's life at stake. Little does she know that this is only the beginning.

Brita's visions uncover a trail of murders centered around the historic Route 66. As Brita steps deeper into the world she has been trying to escape, she and Weston are in a race against time to identify the serial killer. This journey threatens to tear apart their lives as well as those closest to them.

Shattered Hearts [Book 2]

In *Shattered Hearts* Brita Madison's newfound courage is pushed to the limits. A ghost boy she encounters in Phoenix while at a gathering of her new writing clients, who all possess and write about paranormal abilities, ignites an adventure that drags everyone in her world into the dark underbelly of a pedophile ring. Trying to rescue the children puts all of them in the cross-hairs, including her boyfriend Sam and her unofficial partner, James Weston. Many hearts will be shattered before this case is put to rest.

Unraveling Memories [Book 3]

Brita Madison has come a long way since she first met James Weston five years ago. After nearly being killed twice and losing her best friend James at the hand of an evil pedophile, she appreciates the slower pace of her interactions with the spirit world since moving to Phoenix with her new husband, Sam Jenkins. All that comes crashing down when the past returns with a vengeance, threatening her family and friends.

As if to make up for lost time, spirits begin showing up whose muddled memories test the resolve of Brita and her friends, old and new, to meet the challenges from the past and the present.

Circles of Freedom – Contemporary Thriller

When Brandon Boehle creates the Circles of Freedom blogs to strike a blow for truth, he has no idea of the loss, the love, and, the chaos it will set in motion. When the dominoes start to topple, there's a race to survive for friend and foe alike.

Brandon never imagines that a mercenary hired by the President of the United States would be out to kill not only him, but his assistant, Alise Winston, and the professionals who are writing the blogs. What started out as a simple, though carefully safeguarded, effort to get the truth out there has put all of them in the crosshairs. He quickly realizes that his expectations of the United States government have been naïve.

The contract put out on Circles of Freedom turns out to be the least of the worries for the country. A nefarious plot is uncovered to overthrow the government, and the players believe themselves to be untouchable. Circumstances draw Brandon and Alise and all those closest to them into this dark plot. Their only hope lies in a twist of fate.

When the Walls Come Tumbling Down – Women's Fiction

When the Walls Come Tumbling Down is a touching, page-turning novel of triumph over fears and sorrows. As it unfolds, it reminds us that when a crack appears in our walls and widens, something new has a chance to appear.

Two generations apart, Ashley Stanford and Claire Montoya have very little in common until their universes collide. Each has built walls in their life to survive. Ashley, however, has a head start of nearly six decades over Claire as a brick mason of the psyche. Tragedy has brought them together.

For well over a decade, Ashley has been the caregiver for her husband, who now lives in a nursing home. Trying to rediscover her life, she meets Claire, who is homeless and being stalked by a local drug dealer for reporting him to the police. Ashley takes her in and soon discovers there is much more to her story than she could have imagined.

After committing to helping Claire, Ashley is faced with her husband's passing. To help her occupy her mind in her grief, Ashley joins Claire on a journey that could turn both their lives upside down.

The Elyrian Emergence – Science Fiction

Elyria is the only country on the planet of Galen which is located in the Andromeda Galaxy. Galen meaning *calm* and Elyria meaning *blessed place* demonstrate the principles upon which this civilization was founded many centuries ago. Escaping from their ancient planet before it imploded as the result of their destructive policies, the mission of the Founders, those who orchestrated the means of escape, was to develop a civilization based on the philosophy of Self-Emergence.

On the surface, it seems to be working until the Karons, the sensitives who monitor the global energies, detect a negative shift in consciousness. The Karons' visions wake those in charge from their complacency and send them scrambling to curb the decline engineered by someone with an inordinate amount of power.

The questions this team of people find themselves asking are these: *Can we stop this before it's too late? How could we have not seen how vulnerable we are?*

The ultimate question is whether Elyria will wake up and realize that Self-Emergence is a forever journey, one where fear of the mistakes made by the ancient planet have no place if they are going to survive.

Invisible Shadows – Contemporary Thriller

Marriage, even dating, is not on Allegra Harris' list of goals until she meets Harper Frost during a land deal negotiation. A top-notch negotiator, Allegra is justifiably proud of having reached the position of Senior Vice-President of Security Land Investments. Harper's deal falls through, so she's startled when Harper keeps asking her out even though she has no time for relationships. Harper turns out to be as career-focused as she, and the two of them fall into an easy rhythm and ultimately marriage.

Having felt alone most of her life, Allegra doesn't recognize the superficiality of their marriage. She feels content because neither makes demands on the other's time, that is, until Allegra discovers she is pregnant. For the first time, she experiences a love that actively competes for the attention she's always reserved for her work. Chloe's birth shines a new light on hers and Harper's lives and creates a shift in their marriage, but she still believes she loves Harper. Still, the earlier loss of her nest egg to shore up his business lingers in the back of her mind as her need to protect her daughter's future grows.

Everything moves along routinely until the day Allegra receives a phone call from the NTSB. It seems Harper is presumed dead in a plane crash in the Atlantic Ocean while on a flight to Nassau. With no body found, Allegra's life is turned upside down. Trying to handle his affairs, she discovers she did not know her husband at all. The more she tries to tie up loose ends, the more stray threads she discovers. Threads that lead to more questions: Did Harper Frost ever really exist? Is he still alive? Is he dangerous?

Descriptions of My Nonfiction Books

MindSlap!

Is your life making you miserable? Make the move to a better life by learning how to make the creative process work for you! ***You need a method that works no matter what your goal.***

Just because an approach worked for someone else doesn't mean it's going to work for you! You are unique! Your background, your relationships, your education, your experiences all contribute to a wonderfully unique YOU. They influence your thinking and the way you approach the systems that are supposed to make you successful. Most important, however, you need ***a system that allows you to master your intentions.***

Why is it so important to master your intentions? Your Life Intentions are those intentions that are in harmony with your vibration in this life experience. Your Life Intentions are the basis for all that makes you unique.

When you create goals in your life that are expressions of your life intentions, you not only experience greater joy and greater prosperity, but you are taking a path that will bring you full circle to the understanding of how unique you REALLY ARE! Who are you behind all those erroneous thoughts about yourself? You are a powerful, creative being! To use this power for its greatest purpose, you have to be aware of your creations. ***You cannot discover your life's purpose without becoming a conscious creator.***

This brings us back to finding the best method for doing this. You're not looking for a Life Method. You need a method that is spiritually based and allows you to work effectively with your inner psychology.

You need a method that is the driving force behind the Law of Attraction. In *MindSlap!* we offer you a process that is outlined in sacred texts back to ancient times. However, the messages, such as those in the parables, are esoteric or hidden beneath the surface circumstances. It was given this way for those who are ready to dig deeper and take on the mantle of Spirit. ***The 7-Step creative process in this book is the esoteric engine that will move your dreams forward!***

This is the process that enables you to work on letting go of all that isn't serving you. It helps you manifest the goals that express your Life Intentions. Every time you use it, you hone your skills and enhance your inherent abilities – all of which takes you closer and closer to your ultimate goal:

- being at one with the understanding that you and God are One
- accepting your creative birthright and mastering your Life Intentions
- consciously co-creating with God.

Please be aware that *MindSlap!* is the paperback version of a 5 CD audiobook titled *It's Your Move! Transform Your Dreams from Wishful Thinking to Reality*. It was a Bronze Award Winner in ForeWord Magazine's 2004 Book of the Year Awards. There is a very limited supply remaining, but as long as they last, you can contact me at dannyewilliamsen@gmail.com to order for a reduced price: $20 + shipping (US only).

Metaphysical Minute – Philosophy on the Run

Metaphysical Minute is a breath of fresh air in the saturated field of personal evolution. Clarity, insight, and passion punctuate these powerful essays on the concepts that form the foundation for everyone's journey toward spiritual understanding.

Metaphysics is simply an approach to self-knowledge that reaches beyond the belief that it is what we do that is important. It searches always for the path that creates healing within one's soul.

Here are a few of the comments by readers:

"My "Chicken Soup" for Spiritual and Personal Growth. Metaphysical Minute - Philosophy on the Run by Dannye Williamsen is a wonderful tool if you are looking for personal and spiritual growth. This book contains a collection of essays that are not, by any means, a fast, easy read, but an intensely deep, thought provoking look at the way we, as people, look at situations surrounding us and the way we deal with them. I highly recommend reading one essay at a time and then taking time to ponder on the message within it." – S. Wolters

"Metaphysical Minute is a deep, spiritual, and insightful collection of essays that will make you think and define how to live your life to the fullest. I absolutely love it!" – Katia Lord

"I love your book. It feels like my heart's talking!" – Amber Zain

Where Do I Go From Here?

Does it feel like life has let you down? It can be so discouraging when you have worked hard and seen no real return. Your life can begin to cycle between hope and disappointment until you feel that nothing works for you. You see those around you prospering, and you can't understand it. Why not me? you ask.

Then you wake up one morning and ask an age-old question: Where do I go from here? You thought you were on your right path, expressing your passion, but it seems to have fallen on deaf ears.

Whether you're young, old, or somewhere in-between, this moment is when you can make the greatest decision of your life. Stop looking to life for your answers. Clean the lens through which you view life. Examine your inner world as you move forward.

Life Untwisted–Targeting Your Potential with a Fearless Attitude

In trying to live our lives, we inadvertently get things twisted around. We lose sight of what is important for our spiritual growth and what is inconsequential.

Of course, nothing is really inconsequential because lessons are there to be learned regardless. However, it is still important for us to prioritize the people, the actions, the feelings, the thoughts in our lives because most of us tend to turn our worlds upside down. We make the least important the most important and vice versa. We carry the residue of experiences around with us that we should have released long ago and let them rule our lives.

In order to live a happier life, we must learn how to develop a fearless attitude and how to target our potential. Each of these undertakings involves certain areas of work. To develop a fearless attitude, we must work on building a foundation, healing, and strategies, each of which also include many areas of focus. To target our potential, we must understand the creative process, develop visions for our life and business as well as learn how to create better relationships.

A Weary Traveler

Yes, I am a weary traveler at seven decades into my life. I am still searching, and it may seem from the words that flow from me that there is a lack of faith. There isn't. It is just the weariness that can come from traveling the paths we choose for ourselves even though we say we don't want to be on them. Yet, here they are. Some paths are personal. Some are part of the groups of humans with which we identify.

My words sometimes reflect a personal venting; other times an awareness of truth that holds for all of us; and sometimes simply personal observations of the world around me. I can only continue to search for a higher understanding because growing is not an option for me.

The Book of Metanoia

I have consciously been on my spiritual journey for over 40 years. Since the turn of the century, I have been expressing myself through writing. These bits of wisdom came out of my own experiences at different times over these years. I am thrilled to share them with you. If you read my first two novels, you will recognize a few of them that I included there and attributed to the Book of Metanoia, which was only a work in progress at the time.

The Seasons of My Soul – a Poetic Diary

I won't pretend these poems have any value to the literary world because I'm quite sure they don't. They were simply my way of expressing the emotions that were overtaking me at different times in my life and yet filling me with wonder at other times.

I won't apologize if their structure falls short because these "poems" were my safety valve—the outlet that let me release my unproductive emotions. They were also the way I was able to express my personal growth when those around me did not see things the same way I did. So, I bless them. . .warts and all!

As you read the poems, you will notice that I have given you the date each was actually written, beginning in 1963 when I was 14 years old. I also shared the event or attitude that sparked the poem. After I discovered these expressions of mine tucked in-between the boxes and boxes of paper I had accumulated over the years, I instinctively put them in chronological order. That was when I realized it was an order that defined my spiritual journey with all its ups and downs, lessons ignored, and lessons learned. So, at the top of each poem, you will see a running commentary. It is psychological in nature. With hindsight and hopefully greater wisdom, I have tried to present an inner perspective, showing my true journey from 1963 through the poem I wrote when I reached fifty.

Friends who have read my compilation have uniformly told me that even though I had different experiences than some of them, they still recognized the emotions behind the different poems. They said that some evoked memories while others stirred up emotions they thought they had resolved.

Whatever their effect on you, please know that I lay no claim to being a poet. I do believe, however, that we are all one, struggling to express ourselves and experiencing the same emotions with differing circumstances. If my journey helps you in any way, I am simply grateful.

www.ingramcontent.com/pod-product-compliance
Lightning Source LLC
La Vergne TN
LVHW010612100826
845148LV00014B/2931

* 9 7 8 0 9 7 2 6 0 5 8 3 0 *